C-3892   CAREER EXAMINATION SERIES

This is your
PASSBOOK for...

Housing Specialist

Test Preparation Study Guide
Questions & Answers

NATIONAL LEARNING CORPORATION®

COPYRIGHT NOTICE

This book is SOLELY intended for, is sold ONLY to, and its use is RESTRICTED to individual, bona fide applicants or candidates who qualify by virtue of having seriously filed applications for appropriate license, certificate, professional and/or promotional advancement, higher school matriculation, scholarship, or other legitimate requirements of education and/or governmental authorities.

This book is NOT intended for use, class instruction, tutoring, training, duplication, copying, reprinting, excerption, or adaptation, etc., by:

1) Other publishers
2) Proprietors and/or Instructors of "Coaching" and/or Preparatory Courses
3) Personnel and/or Training Divisions of commercial, industrial, and governmental organizations
4) Schools, colleges, or universities and/or their departments and staffs, including teachers and other personnel
5) Testing Agencies or Bureaus
6) Study groups which seek by the purchase of a single volume to copy and/or duplicate and/or adapt this material for use by the group as a whole without having purchased individual volumes for each of the members of the group
7) Et al.

Such persons would be in violation of appropriate Federal and State statutes.

PROVISION OF LICENSING AGREEMENTS – Recognized educational, commercial, industrial, and governmental institutions and organizations, and others legitimately engaged in educational pursuits, including training, testing, and measurement activities, may address request for a licensing agreement to the copyright owners, who will determine whether, and under what conditions, including fees and charges, the materials in this book may be used them. In other words, a licensing facility exists for the legitimate use of the material in this book on other than an individual basis. However, it is asseverated and affirmed here that the material in this book CANNOT be used without the receipt of the express permission of such a licensing agreement from the Publishers. Inquiries re licensing should be addressed to the company, attention rights and permissions department.

All rights reserved, including the right of reproduction in whole or in part, in any form or by any means, electronic or mechanical, including photocopying, recording, or by any information storage and retrieval system, without permission in writing from the Publisher.

Copyright © 2025 by
National Learning Corporation

212 Michael Drive, Syosset, NY 11791
(516) 921-8888 • www.passbooks.com
E-mail: info@passbooks.com

PASSBOOK® SERIES

THE *PASSBOOK® SERIES* has been created to prepare applicants and candidates for the ultimate academic battlefield – the examination room.

At some time in our lives, each and every one of us may be required to take an examination – for validation, matriculation, admission, qualification, registration, certification, or licensure.

Based on the assumption that every applicant or candidate has met the basic formal educational standards, has taken the required number of courses, and read the necessary texts, the *PASSBOOK® SERIES* furnishes the one special preparation which may assure passing with confidence, instead of failing with insecurity. Examination questions – together with answers – are furnished as the basic vehicle for study so that the mysteries of the examination and its compounding difficulties may be eliminated or diminished by a sure method.

This book is meant to help you pass your examination provided that you qualify and are serious in your objective.

The entire field is reviewed through the huge store of content information which is succinctly presented through a provocative and challenging approach – the question-and-answer method.

A climate of success is established by furnishing the correct answers at the end of each test.

You soon learn to recognize types of questions, forms of questions, and patterns of questioning. You may even begin to anticipate expected outcomes.

You perceive that many questions are repeated or adapted so that you can gain acute insights, which may enable you to score many sure points.

You learn how to confront new questions, or types of questions, and to attack them confidently and work out the correct answers.

You note objectives and emphases, and recognize pitfalls and dangers, so that you may make positive educational adjustments.

Moreover, you are kept fully informed in relation to new concepts, methods, practices, and directions in the field.

You discover that you are actually taking the examination all the time: you are preparing for the examination by "taking" an examination, not by reading extraneous and/or supererogatory textbooks.

In short, this PASSBOOK®, used directedly, should be an important factor in helping you to pass your test.

HOUSING SPECIALIST

DUTIES:
A Housing Specialist provides technical assistance to municipalities for the development of housing and community development programs;

- Prepares the Housing Assistance Plan and tables of the County's Housing and Committee Development Application;
- Renders technical assistance to municipalities upon request regarding such issues as a revolving rehabilitation fund, federally-assisted housing, provides assistance through seminars and on individual municipal basis;
- As assigned, attends meetings, especially those conducted by municipalities, to make presentations and make recommendations, regarding housing programs incurred in the Housing and Community Development and regarding such housing-related projects for which municipalities may request County technical assistance;
- Assists senior staff members in the conceptualization of an information data system through which to inform participant municipalities regarding housing programs;
- Will collect, analyze, organize and distribute such information; carries out such field work as may be necessary to gather primary data (i.e. surveys, windshield surveys, etc.), and to provide technical counsel;
- Assists the Director in maintaining working liaison with housing and housing-related agencies assists the division of Planning as required.

SUBJECTS OF THE EXAMINATION:
The written test is designed to evaluate knowledge, skills and/or abilities in the following areas:

1. **Interviewing** - These questions test for knowledge of the principles and practices employed in obtaining information from individuals through structured conversations. These questions require you to apply the principles, practices, and techniques of effective interviewing to hypothetical interviewing situations. Included are questions that present a problem arising from an interviewing situation, and you must choose the most appropriate course of action to take.
2. **Preparing written material** - These questions test for the ability to present information clearly and accurately, and to organize paragraphs logically and comprehensibly. For some questions, you will be given information in two or three sentences followed by four restatements of the information. You must then choose the best version. For other questions, you will be given paragraphs with their sentences out of order. You must then choose, from four suggestions, the best order for the sentences.
3. **Understanding and interpreting numerical data related to community development and housing** - These questions test for the ability to understand and interpret numerical data related to community development and housing. The data will be presented in formats such as tables and charts. All the information needed to answer the questions will be provided in the data presented. You may be required to perform basic mathematical functions such as addition, subtraction, multiplication, and division and to calculate averages and percentages. You should bring with you a hand-held battery- or solar-powered calculator for use on this test. You will not be permitted to use the calculator function of your cell phone or other electronic devices.
4. **Understanding, interpreting and applying housing and community development laws, rules and regulations** - These questions test for the ability to understand, interpret, and apply a variety of federal and State housing and community development laws, rules, and regulations. You will be provided with a brief reading selection based on or extracted from a passage of legal text. You must read the selection and then answer one or more questions based on that selection. All the information needed to answer the questions will be provided in the reading selections.

HOW TO TAKE A TEST

I. YOU MUST PASS AN EXAMINATION

A. *WHAT EVERY CANDIDATE SHOULD KNOW*

Examination applicants often ask us for help in preparing for the written test. What can I study in advance? What kinds of questions will be asked? How will the test be given? How will the papers be graded?

As an applicant for a civil service examination, you may be wondering about some of these things. Our purpose here is to suggest effective methods of advance study and to describe civil service examinations.

Your chances for success on this examination can be increased if you know how to prepare. Those "pre-examination jitters" can be reduced if you know what to expect. You can even experience an adventure in good citizenship if you know why civil service exams are given.

B. *WHY ARE CIVIL SERVICE EXAMINATIONS GIVEN?*

Civil service examinations are important to you in two ways. As a citizen, you want public jobs filled by employees who know how to do their work. As a job seeker, you want a fair chance to compete for that job on an equal footing with other candidates. The best-known means of accomplishing this two-fold goal is the competitive examination.

Exams are widely publicized throughout the nation. They may be administered for jobs in federal, state, city, municipal, town or village governments or agencies.

Any citizen may apply, with some limitations, such as the age or residence of applicants. Your experience and education may be reviewed to see whether you meet the requirements for the particular examination. When these requirements exist, they are reasonable and applied consistently to all applicants. Thus, a competitive examination may cause you some uneasiness now, but it is your privilege and safeguard.

C. *HOW ARE CIVIL SERVICE EXAMS DEVELOPED?*

Examinations are carefully written by trained technicians who are specialists in the field known as "psychological measurement," in consultation with recognized authorities in the field of work that the test will cover. These experts recommend the subject matter areas or skills to be tested; only those knowledges or skills important to your success on the job are included. The most reliable books and source materials available are used as references. Together, the experts and technicians judge the difficulty level of the questions.

Test technicians know how to phrase questions so that the problem is clearly stated. Their ethics do not permit "trick" or "catch" questions. Questions may have been tried out on sample groups, or subjected to statistical analysis, to determine their usefulness.

Written tests are often used in combination with performance tests, ratings of training and experience, and oral interviews. All of these measures combine to form the best-known means of finding the right person for the right job.

II. HOW TO PASS THE WRITTEN TEST

A. NATURE OF THE EXAMINATION

To prepare intelligently for civil service examinations, you should know how they differ from school examinations you have taken. In school you were assigned certain definite pages to read or subjects to cover. The examination questions were quite detailed and usually emphasized memory. Civil service exams, on the other hand, try to discover your present ability to perform the duties of a position, plus your potentiality to learn these duties. In other words, a civil service exam attempts to predict how successful you will be. Questions cover such a broad area that they cannot be as minute and detailed as school exam questions.

In the public service similar kinds of work, or positions, are grouped together in one "class." This process is known as *position-classification*. All the positions in a class are paid according to the salary range for that class. One class title covers all of these positions, and they are all tested by the same examination.

B. FOUR BASIC STEPS

1) Study the announcement

How, then, can you know what subjects to study? Our best answer is: "Learn as much as possible about the class of positions for which you've applied." The exam will test the knowledge, skills and abilities needed to do the work.

Your most valuable source of information about the position you want is the official exam announcement. This announcement lists the training and experience qualifications. Check these standards and apply only if you come reasonably close to meeting them.

The brief description of the position in the examination announcement offers some clues to the subjects which will be tested. Think about the job itself. Review the duties in your mind. Can you perform them, or are there some in which you are rusty? Fill in the blank spots in your preparation.

Many jurisdictions preview the written test in the exam announcement by including a section called "Knowledge and Abilities Required," "Scope of the Examination," or some similar heading. Here you will find out specifically what fields will be tested.

2) Review your own background

Once you learn in general what the position is all about, and what you need to know to do the work, ask yourself which subjects you already know fairly well and which need improvement. You may wonder whether to concentrate on improving your strong areas or on building some background in your fields of weakness. When the announcement has specified "some knowledge" or "considerable knowledge," or has used adjectives like "beginning principles of…" or "advanced … methods," you can get a clue as to the number and difficulty of questions to be asked in any given field. More questions, and hence broader coverage, would be included for those subjects which are more important in the work. Now weigh your strengths and weaknesses against the job requirements and prepare accordingly.

3) Determine the level of the position

Another way to tell how intensively you should prepare is to understand the level of the job for which you are applying. Is it the entering level? In other words, is this the position in which beginners in a field of work are hired? Or is it an intermediate or advanced level? Sometimes this is indicated by such words as "Junior" or "Senior" in the class title. Other jurisdictions use Roman numerals to designate the level – Clerk I, Clerk II, for example. The word "Supervisor" sometimes appears in the title. If the level is not indicated by the title, check the description of duties. Will you be working under very close supervision, or will you have responsibility for independent decisions in this work?

4) Choose appropriate study materials

Now that you know the subjects to be examined and the relative amount of each subject to be covered, you can choose suitable study materials. For beginning level jobs, or even advanced ones, if you have a pronounced weakness in some aspect of your training, read a modern, standard textbook in that field. Be sure it is up to date and has general coverage. Such books are normally available at your library, and the librarian will be glad to help you locate one. For entry-level positions, questions of appropriate difficulty are chosen – neither highly advanced questions, nor those too simple. Such questions require careful thought but not advanced training.

If the position for which you are applying is technical or advanced, you will read more advanced, specialized material. If you are already familiar with the basic principles of your field, elementary textbooks would waste your time. Concentrate on advanced textbooks and technical periodicals. Think through the concepts and review difficult problems in your field.

These are all general sources. You can get more ideas on your own initiative, following these leads. For example, training manuals and publications of the government agency which employs workers in your field can be useful, particularly for technical and professional positions. A letter or visit to the government department involved may result in more specific study suggestions, and certainly will provide you with a more definite idea of the exact nature of the position you are seeking.

III. KINDS OF TESTS

Tests are used for purposes other than measuring knowledge and ability to perform specified duties. For some positions, it is equally important to test ability to make adjustments to new situations or to profit from training. In others, basic mental abilities not dependent on information are essential. Questions which test these things may not appear as pertinent to the duties of the position as those which test for knowledge and information. Yet they are often highly important parts of a fair examination. For very general questions, it is almost impossible to help you direct your study efforts. What we can do is to point out some of the more common of these general abilities needed in public service positions and describe some typical questions.

1) General information

Broad, general information has been found useful for predicting job success in some kinds of work. This is tested in a variety of ways, from vocabulary lists to questions about current events. Basic background in some field of work, such as sociology or economics, may be sampled in a group of questions. Often these are principles which have become familiar to most persons through exposure rather than through formal training. It is difficult to advise you how to study for these questions; being alert to the world around you is our best suggestion.

2) Verbal ability

An example of an ability needed in many positions is verbal or language ability. Verbal ability is, in brief, the ability to use and understand words. Vocabulary and grammar tests are typical measures of this ability. Reading comprehension or paragraph interpretation questions are common in many kinds of civil service tests. You are given a paragraph of written material and asked to find its central meaning.

3) Numerical ability

Number skills can be tested by the familiar arithmetic problem, by checking paired lists of numbers to see which are alike and which are different, or by interpreting charts and graphs. In the latter test, a graph may be printed in the test booklet which you are asked to use as the basis for answering questions.

4) Observation

A popular test for law-enforcement positions is the observation test. A picture is shown to you for several minutes, then taken away. Questions about the picture test your ability to observe both details and larger elements.

5) Following directions

In many positions in the public service, the employee must be able to carry out written instructions dependably and accurately. You may be given a chart with several columns, each column listing a variety of information. The questions require you to carry out directions involving the information given in the chart.

6) Skills and aptitudes

Performance tests effectively measure some manual skills and aptitudes. When the skill is one in which you are trained, such as typing or shorthand, you can practice. These tests are often very much like those given in business school or high school courses. For many of the other skills and aptitudes, however, no short-time preparation can be made. Skills and abilities natural to you or that you have developed throughout your lifetime are being tested.

Many of the general questions just described provide all the data needed to answer the questions and ask you to use your reasoning ability to find the answers. Your best preparation for these tests, as well as for tests of facts and ideas, is to be at your physical and mental best. You, no doubt, have your own methods of getting into an exam-taking mood and keeping "in shape." The next section lists some ideas on this subject.

IV. KINDS OF QUESTIONS

Only rarely is the "essay" question, which you answer in narrative form, used in civil service tests. Civil service tests are usually of the short-answer type. Full instructions for answering these questions will be given to you at the examination. But in case this is your first experience with short-answer questions and separate answer sheets, here is what you need to know:

1) Multiple-choice Questions

Most popular of the short-answer questions is the "multiple choice" or "best answer" question. It can be used, for example, to test for factual knowledge, ability to solve problems or judgment in meeting situations found at work.

A multiple-choice question is normally one of three types—
- It can begin with an incomplete statement followed by several possible endings. You are to find the one ending which *best* completes the statement, although some of the others may not be entirely wrong.
- It can also be a complete statement in the form of a question which is answered by choosing one of the statements listed.

- It can be in the form of a problem – again you select the best answer.

Here is an example of a multiple-choice question with a discussion which should give you some clues as to the method for choosing the right answer:

When an employee has a complaint about his assignment, the action which will *best* help him overcome his difficulty is to
    A. discuss his difficulty with his coworkers
    B. take the problem to the head of the organization
    C. take the problem to the person who gave him the assignment
    D. say nothing to anyone about his complaint

In answering this question, you should study each of the choices to find which is best. Consider choice "A" – Certainly an employee may discuss his complaint with fellow employees, but no change or improvement can result, and the complaint remains unresolved. Choice "B" is a poor choice since the head of the organization probably does not know what assignment you have been given, and taking your problem to him is known as "going over the head" of the supervisor. The supervisor, or person who made the assignment, is the person who can clarify it or correct any injustice. Choice "C" is, therefore, correct. To say nothing, as in choice "D," is unwise. Supervisors have and interest in knowing the problems employees are facing, and the employee is seeking a solution to his problem.

2) True/False Questions

The "true/false" or "right/wrong" form of question is sometimes used. Here a complete statement is given. Your job is to decide whether the statement is right or wrong.

SAMPLE: A roaming cell-phone call to a nearby city costs less than a non-roaming call to a distant city.

This statement is wrong, or false, since roaming calls are more expensive.
This is not a complete list of all possible question forms, although most of the others are variations of these common types. You will always get complete directions for answering questions. Be sure you understand *how* to mark your answers – ask questions until you do.

V. RECORDING YOUR ANSWERS

Computer terminals are used more and more today for many different kinds of exams.
For an examination with very few applicants, you may be told to record your answers in the test booklet itself. Separate answer sheets are much more common. If this separate answer sheet is to be scored by machine – and this is often the case – it is highly important that you mark your answers correctly in order to get credit.
An electronic scoring machine is often used in civil service offices because of the speed with which papers can be scored. Machine-scored answer sheets must be marked with a pencil, which will be given to you. This pencil has a high graphite content which responds to the electronic scoring machine. As a matter of fact, stray dots may register as answers, so do not let your pencil rest on the answer sheet while you are pondering the correct answer. Also, if your pencil lead breaks or is otherwise defective, ask for another.

Since the answer sheet will be dropped in a slot in the scoring machine, be careful not to bend the corners or get the paper crumpled.

The answer sheet normally has five vertical columns of numbers, with 30 numbers to a column. These numbers correspond to the question numbers in your test booklet. After each number, going across the page are four or five pairs of dotted lines. These short dotted lines have small letters or numbers above them. The first two pairs may also have a "T" or "F" above the letters. This indicates that the first two pairs only are to be used if the questions are of the true-false type. If the questions are multiple choice, disregard the "T" and "F" and pay attention only to the small letters or numbers.

Answer your questions in the manner of the sample that follows:

32. The largest city in the United States is
    A. Washington, D.C.
    B. New York City
    C. Chicago
    D. Detroit
    E. San Francisco

1) Choose the answer you think is best. (New York City is the largest, so "B" is correct.)
2) Find the row of dotted lines numbered the same as the question you are answering. (Find row number 32)
3) Find the pair of dotted lines corresponding to the answer. (Find the pair of lines under the mark "B.")
4) Make a solid black mark between the dotted lines.

VI. BEFORE THE TEST

Common sense will help you find procedures to follow to get ready for an examination. Too many of us, however, overlook these sensible measures. Indeed, nervousness and fatigue have been found to be the most serious reasons why applicants fail to do their best on civil service tests. Here is a list of reminders:

- Begin your preparation early – Don't wait until the last minute to go scurrying around for books and materials or to find out what the position is all about.
- Prepare continuously – An hour a night for a week is better than an all-night cram session. This has been definitely established. What is more, a night a week for a month will return better dividends than crowding your study into a shorter period of time.
- Locate the place of the exam – You have been sent a notice telling you when and where to report for the examination. If the location is in a different town or otherwise unfamiliar to you, it would be well to inquire the best route and learn something about the building.
- Relax the night before the test – Allow your mind to rest. Do not study at all that night. Plan some mild recreation or diversion; then go to bed early and get a good night's sleep.
- Get up early enough to make a leisurely trip to the place for the test – This way unforeseen events, traffic snarls, unfamiliar buildings, etc. will not upset you.
- Dress comfortably – A written test is not a fashion show. You will be known by number and not by name, so wear something comfortable.

- Leave excess paraphernalia at home – Shopping bags and odd bundles will get in your way. You need bring only the items mentioned in the official notice you received; usually everything you need is provided. Do not bring reference books to the exam. They will only confuse those last minutes and be taken away from you when in the test room.
- Arrive somewhat ahead of time – If because of transportation schedules you must get there very early, bring a newspaper or magazine to take your mind off yourself while waiting.
- Locate the examination room – When you have found the proper room, you will be directed to the seat or part of the room where you will sit. Sometimes you are given a sheet of instructions to read while you are waiting. Do not fill out any forms until you are told to do so; just read them and be prepared.
- Relax and prepare to listen to the instructions
- If you have any physical problem that may keep you from doing your best, be sure to tell the test administrator. If you are sick or in poor health, you really cannot do your best on the exam. You can come back and take the test some other time.

VII. AT THE TEST

The day of the test is here and you have the test booklet in your hand. The temptation to get going is very strong. Caution! There is more to success than knowing the right answers. You must know how to identify your papers and understand variations in the type of short-answer question used in this particular examination. Follow these suggestions for maximum results from your efforts:

1) Cooperate with the monitor

The test administrator has a duty to create a situation in which you can be as much at ease as possible. He will give instructions, tell you when to begin, check to see that you are marking your answer sheet correctly, and so on. He is not there to guard you, although he will see that your competitors do not take unfair advantage. He wants to help you do your best.

2) Listen to all instructions

Don't jump the gun! Wait until you understand all directions. In most civil service tests you get more time than you need to answer the questions. So don't be in a hurry. Read each word of instructions until you clearly understand the meaning. Study the examples, listen to all announcements and follow directions. Ask questions if you do not understand what to do.

3) Identify your papers

Civil service exams are usually identified by number only. You will be assigned a number; you must not put your name on your test papers. Be sure to copy your number correctly. Since more than one exam may be given, copy your exact examination title.

4) Plan your time

Unless you are told that a test is a "speed" or "rate of work" test, speed itself is usually not important. Time enough to answer all the questions will be provided, but this does not mean that you have all day. An overall time limit has been set. Divide the total time (in minutes) by the number of questions to determine the approximate time you have for each question.

5) Do not linger over difficult questions

If you come across a difficult question, mark it with a paper clip (useful to have along) and come back to it when you have been through the booklet. One caution if you do this – be sure to skip a number on your answer sheet as well. Check often to be sure that you have not lost your place and that you are marking in the row numbered the same as the question you are answering.

6) Read the questions

Be sure you know what the question asks! Many capable people are unsuccessful because they failed to *read* the questions correctly.

7) Answer all questions

Unless you have been instructed that a penalty will be deducted for incorrect answers, it is better to guess than to omit a question.

8) Speed tests

It is often better NOT to guess on speed tests. It has been found that on timed tests people are tempted to spend the last few seconds before time is called in marking answers at random – without even reading them – in the hope of picking up a few extra points. To discourage this practice, the instructions may warn you that your score will be "corrected" for guessing. That is, a penalty will be applied. The incorrect answers will be deducted from the correct ones, or some other penalty formula will be used.

9) Review your answers

If you finish before time is called, go back to the questions you guessed or omitted to give them further thought. Review other answers if you have time.

10) Return your test materials

If you are ready to leave before others have finished or time is called, take ALL your materials to the monitor and leave quietly. Never take any test material with you. The monitor can discover whose papers are not complete, and taking a test booklet may be grounds for disqualification.

VIII. EXAMINATION TECHNIQUES

1) Read the general instructions carefully. These are usually printed on the first page of the exam booklet. As a rule, these instructions refer to the timing of the examination; the fact that you should not start work until the signal and must stop work at a signal, etc. If there are any *special* instructions, such as a choice of questions to be answered, make sure that you note this instruction carefully.

2) When you are ready to start work on the examination, that is as soon as the signal has been given, read the instructions to each question booklet, underline any key words or phrases, such as *least, best, outline, describe* and the like. In this way you will tend to answer as requested rather than discover on reviewing your paper that you *listed without describing*, that you selected the *worst* choice rather than the *best* choice, etc.

3) If the examination is of the objective or multiple-choice type – that is, each question will also give a series of possible answers: A, B, C or D, and you are called upon to select the best answer and write the letter next to that answer on your answer paper – it is advisable to start answering each question in turn. There may be anywhere from 50 to 100 such questions in the three or four hours allotted and you can see how much time would be taken if you read through all the questions before beginning to answer any. Furthermore, if you come across a question or group of questions which you know would be difficult to answer, it would undoubtedly affect your handling of all the other questions.

4) If the examination is of the essay type and contains but a few questions, it is a moot point as to whether you should read all the questions before starting to answer any one. Of course, if you are given a choice – say five out of seven and the like – then it is essential to read all the questions so you can eliminate the two that are most difficult. If, however, you are asked to answer all the questions, there may be danger in trying to answer the easiest one first because you may find that you will spend too much time on it. The best technique is to answer the first question, then proceed to the second, etc.

5) Time your answers. Before the exam begins, write down the time it started, then add the time allowed for the examination and write down the time it must be completed, then divide the time available somewhat as follows:
    - If 3-1/2 hours are allowed, that would be 210 minutes. If you have 80 objective-type questions, that would be an average of 2-1/2 minutes per question. Allow yourself no more than 2 minutes per question, or a total of 160 minutes, which will permit about 50 minutes to review.
    - If for the time allotment of 210 minutes there are 7 essay questions to answer, that would average about 30 minutes a question. Give yourself only 25 minutes per question so that you have about 35 minutes to review.

6) The most important instruction is to *read each question* and make sure you know what is wanted. The second most important instruction is to *time yourself properly* so that you answer every question. The third most important instruction is to *answer every question*. Guess if you have to but include something for each question. Remember that you will receive no credit for a blank and will probably receive some credit if you write something in answer to an essay question. If you guess a letter – say "B" for a multiple-choice question – you may have guessed right. If you leave a blank as an answer to a multiple-choice question, the examiners may respect your feelings but it will not add a point to your score. Some exams may penalize you for wrong answers, so in such cases *only*, you may not want to guess unless you have some basis for your answer.

7) Suggestions
    a. Objective-type questions
        1. Examine the question booklet for proper sequence of pages and questions
        2. Read all instructions carefully
        3. Skip any question which seems too difficult; return to it after all other questions have been answered
        4. Apportion your time properly; do not spend too much time on any single question or group of questions

5. Note and underline key words – *all, most, fewest, least, best, worst, same, opposite*, etc.
6. Pay particular attention to negatives
7. Note unusual option, e.g., unduly long, short, complex, different or similar in content to the body of the question
8. Observe the use of "hedging" words – *probably, may, most likely*, etc.
9. Make sure that your answer is put next to the same number as the question
10. Do not second-guess unless you have good reason to believe the second answer is definitely more correct
11. Cross out original answer if you decide another answer is more accurate; do not erase until you are ready to hand your paper in
12. Answer all questions; guess unless instructed otherwise
13. Leave time for review

b. Essay questions
   1. Read each question carefully
   2. Determine exactly what is wanted. Underline key words or phrases.
   3. Decide on outline or paragraph answer
   4. Include many different points and elements unless asked to develop any one or two points or elements
   5. Show impartiality by giving pros and cons unless directed to select one side only
   6. Make and write down any assumptions you find necessary to answer the questions
   7. Watch your English, grammar, punctuation and choice of words
   8. Time your answers; don't crowd material

8) Answering the essay question

Most essay questions can be answered by framing the specific response around several key words or ideas. Here are a few such key words or ideas:

M's: manpower, materials, methods, money, management
P's: purpose, program, policy, plan, procedure, practice, problems, pitfalls, personnel, public relations
   a. Six basic steps in handling problems:
      1. Preliminary plan and background development
      2. Collect information, data and facts
      3. Analyze and interpret information, data and facts
      4. Analyze and develop solutions as well as make recommendations
      5. Prepare report and sell recommendations
      6. Install recommendations and follow up effectiveness

   b. Pitfalls to avoid
      1. *Taking things for granted* – A statement of the situation does not necessarily imply that each of the elements is necessarily true; for example, a complaint may be invalid and biased so that all that can be taken for granted is that a complaint has been registered

2. *Considering only one side of a situation* – Wherever possible, indicate several alternatives and then point out the reasons you selected the best one
3. *Failing to indicate follow up* – Whenever your answer indicates action on your part, make certain that you will take proper follow-up action to see how successful your recommendations, procedures or actions turn out to be
4. *Taking too long in answering any single question* – Remember to time your answers properly

IX. AFTER THE TEST

Scoring procedures differ in detail among civil service jurisdictions although the general principles are the same. Whether the papers are hand-scored or graded by machine we have described, they are nearly always graded by number. That is, the person who marks the paper knows only the number – never the name – of the applicant. Not until all the papers have been graded will they be matched with names. If other tests, such as training and experience or oral interview ratings have been given, scores will be combined. Different parts of the examination usually have different weights. For example, the written test might count 60 percent of the final grade, and a rating of training and experience 40 percent. In many jurisdictions, veterans will have a certain number of points added to their grades.

After the final grade has been determined, the names are placed in grade order and an eligible list is established. There are various methods for resolving ties between those who get the same final grade – probably the most common is to place first the name of the person whose application was received first. Job offers are made from the eligible list in the order the names appear on it. You will be notified of your grade and your rank as soon as all these computations have been made. This will be done as rapidly as possible.

People who are found to meet the requirements in the announcement are called "eligibles." Their names are put on a list of eligible candidates. An eligible's chances of getting a job depend on how high he stands on this list and how fast agencies are filling jobs from the list.

When a job is to be filled from a list of eligibles, the agency asks for the names of people on the list of eligibles for that job. When the civil service commission receives this request, it sends to the agency the names of the three people highest on this list. Or, if the job to be filled has specialized requirements, the office sends the agency the names of the top three persons who meet these requirements from the general list.

The appointing officer makes a choice from among the three people whose names were sent to him. If the selected person accepts the appointment, the names of the others are put back on the list to be considered for future openings.

That is the rule in hiring from all kinds of eligible lists, whether they are for typist, carpenter, chemist, or something else. For every vacancy, the appointing officer has his choice of any one of the top three eligibles on the list. This explains why the person whose name is on top of the list sometimes does not get an appointment when some of the persons lower on the list do. If the appointing officer chooses the second or third eligible, the No. 1 eligible does not get a job at once, but stays on the list until he is appointed or the list is terminated.

X. HOW TO PASS THE INTERVIEW TEST

The examination for which you applied requires an oral interview test. You have already taken the written test and you are now being called for the interview test – the final part of the formal examination.

You may think that it is not possible to prepare for an interview test and that there are no procedures to follow during an interview. Our purpose is to point out some things you can do in advance that will help you and some good rules to follow and pitfalls to avoid while you are being interviewed.

What is an interview supposed to test?

The written examination is designed to test the technical knowledge and competence of the candidate; the oral is designed to evaluate intangible qualities, not readily measured otherwise, and to establish a list showing the relative fitness of each candidate – as measured against his competitors – for the position sought. Scoring is not on the basis of "right" and "wrong," but on a sliding scale of values ranging from "not passable" to "outstanding." As a matter of fact, it is possible to achieve a relatively low score without a single "incorrect" answer because of evident weakness in the qualities being measured.

Occasionally, an examination may consist entirely of an oral test – either an individual or a group oral. In such cases, information is sought concerning the technical knowledges and abilities of the candidate, since there has been no written examination for this purpose. More commonly, however, an oral test is used to supplement a written examination.

Who conducts interviews?

The composition of oral boards varies among different jurisdictions. In nearly all, a representative of the personnel department serves as chairman. One of the members of the board may be a representative of the department in which the candidate would work. In some cases, "outside experts" are used, and, frequently, a businessman or some other representative of the general public is asked to serve. Labor and management or other special groups may be represented. The aim is to secure the services of experts in the appropriate field.

However the board is composed, it is a good idea (and not at all improper or unethical) to ascertain in advance of the interview who the members are and what groups they represent. When you are introduced to them, you will have some idea of their backgrounds and interests, and at least you will not stutter and stammer over their names.

What should be done before the interview?

While knowledge about the board members is useful and takes some of the surprise element out of the interview, there is other preparation which is more substantive. It *is* possible to prepare for an oral interview – in several ways:

1) Keep a copy of your application and review it carefully before the interview

This may be the only document before the oral board, and the starting point of the interview. Know what education and experience you have listed there, and the sequence and dates of all of it. Sometimes the board will ask you to review the highlights of your experience for them; you should not have to hem and haw doing it.

2) Study the class specification and the examination announcement

Usually, the oral board has one or both of these to guide them. The qualities, characteristics or knowledges required by the position sought are stated in these documents. They offer valuable clues as to the nature of the oral interview. For example, if the job involves supervisory responsibilities, the announcement will usually indicate that knowledge of modern supervisory methods and the qualifications of the candidate as a supervisor will be tested. If so, you can expect such questions, frequently in the form of a hypothetical situation which you are expected to solve. NEVER go into an oral without knowledge of the duties and responsibilities of the job you seek.

3) Think through each qualification required

Try to visualize the kind of questions you would ask if you were a board member. How well could you answer them? Try especially to appraise your own knowledge and background in each area, *measured against the job sought*, and identify any areas in which you are weak. Be critical and realistic – do not flatter yourself.

4) Do some general reading in areas in which you feel you may be weak

For example, if the job involves supervision and your past experience has NOT, some general reading in supervisory methods and practices, particularly in the field of human relations, might be useful. Do NOT study agency procedures or detailed manuals. The oral board will be testing your understanding and capacity, not your memory.

5) Get a good night's sleep and watch your general health and mental attitude

You will want a clear head at the interview. Take care of a cold or any other minor ailment, and of course, no hangovers.

What should be done on the day of the interview?

Now comes the day of the interview itself. Give yourself plenty of time to get there. Plan to arrive somewhat ahead of the scheduled time, particularly if your appointment is in the fore part of the day. If a previous candidate fails to appear, the board might be ready for you a bit early. By early afternoon an oral board is almost invariably behind schedule if there are many candidates, and you may have to wait. Take along a book or magazine to read, or your application to review, but leave any extraneous material in the waiting room when you go in for your interview. In any event, relax and compose yourself.

The matter of dress is important. The board is forming impressions about you – from your experience, your manners, your attitude, and your appearance. Give your personal appearance careful attention. Dress your best, but not your flashiest. Choose conservative, appropriate clothing, and be sure it is immaculate. This is a business interview, and your appearance should indicate that you regard it as such. Besides, being well groomed and properly dressed will help boost your confidence.

Sooner or later, someone will call your name and escort you into the interview room. *This is it.* From here on you are on your own. It is too late for any more preparation. But remember, you asked for this opportunity to prove your fitness, and you are here because your request was granted.

What happens when you go in?

The usual sequence of events will be as follows: The clerk (who is often the board stenographer) will introduce you to the chairman of the oral board, who will introduce you to the other members of the board. Acknowledge the introductions before you sit down. Do not be surprised if you find a microphone facing you or a stenotypist sitting by. Oral interviews are usually recorded in the event of an appeal or other review.

Usually the chairman of the board will open the interview by reviewing the highlights of your education and work experience from your application – primarily for the benefit of the other members of the board, as well as to get the material into the record. Do not interrupt or comment unless there is an error or significant misinterpretation; if that is the case, do not hesitate. But do not quibble about insignificant matters. Also, he will usually ask you some question about your education, experience or your present job – partly to get you to start talking and to establish the interviewing "rapport." He may start the actual questioning, or turn it over to one of the other members. Frequently, each member undertakes the questioning on a particular area, one in which he is perhaps most competent, so you can expect each member to participate in the examination. Because time is limited, you may also expect some rather abrupt switches in the direction the questioning takes, so do not be upset by it. Normally, a board member will not pursue a single line of questioning unless he discovers a particular strength or weakness.

After each member has participated, the chairman will usually ask whether any member has any further questions, then will ask you if you have anything you wish to add. Unless you are expecting this question, it may floor you. Worse, it may start you off on an extended, extemporaneous speech. The board is not usually seeking more information. The question is principally to offer you a last opportunity to present further qualifications or to indicate that you have nothing to add. So, if you feel that a significant qualification or characteristic has been overlooked, it is proper to point it out in a sentence or so. Do not compliment the board on the thoroughness of their examination – they have been sketchy, and you know it. If you wish, merely say, "No thank you, I have nothing further to add." This is a point where you can "talk yourself out" of a good impression or fail to present an important bit of information. Remember, *you close the interview yourself*.

The chairman will then say, "That is all, Mr. _____, thank you." Do not be startled; the interview is over, and quicker than you think. Thank him, gather your belongings and take your leave. Save your sigh of relief for the other side of the door.

How to put your best foot forward

Throughout this entire process, you may feel that the board individually and collectively is trying to pierce your defenses, seek out your hidden weaknesses and embarrass and confuse you. Actually, this is not true. They are obliged to make an appraisal of your qualifications for the job you are seeking, and they want to see you in your best light. Remember, they must interview all candidates and a non-cooperative candidate may become a failure in spite of their best efforts to bring out his qualifications. Here are 15 suggestions that will help you:

1) Be natural – Keep your attitude confident, not cocky

If you are not confident that you can do the job, do not expect the board to be. Do not apologize for your weaknesses, try to bring out your strong points. The board is interested in a positive, not negative, presentation. Cockiness will antagonize any board member and make him wonder if you are covering up a weakness by a false show of strength.

2) Get comfortable, but don't lounge or sprawl

Sit erectly but not stiffly. A careless posture may lead the board to conclude that you are careless in other things, or at least that you are not impressed by the importance of the occasion. Either conclusion is natural, even if incorrect. Do not fuss with your clothing, a pencil or an ashtray. Your hands may occasionally be useful to emphasize a point; do not let them become a point of distraction.

3) Do not wisecrack or make small talk

This is a serious situation, and your attitude should show that you consider it as such. Further, the time of the board is limited – they do not want to waste it, and neither should you.

4) Do not exaggerate your experience or abilities

In the first place, from information in the application or other interviews and sources, the board may know more about you than you think. Secondly, you probably will not get away with it. An experienced board is rather adept at spotting such a situation, so do not take the chance.

5) If you know a board member, do not make a point of it, yet do not hide it

Certainly you are not fooling him, and probably not the other members of the board. Do not try to take advantage of your acquaintanceship – it will probably do you little good.

6) Do not dominate the interview

Let the board do that. They will give you the clues – do not assume that you have to do all the talking. Realize that the board has a number of questions to ask you, and do not try to take up all the interview time by showing off your extensive knowledge of the answer to the first one.

7) Be attentive

You only have 20 minutes or so, and you should keep your attention at its sharpest throughout. When a member is addressing a problem or question to you, give him your undivided attention. Address your reply principally to him, but do not exclude the other board members.

8) Do not interrupt

A board member may be stating a problem for you to analyze. He will ask you a question when the time comes. Let him state the problem, and wait for the question.

9) Make sure you understand the question

Do not try to answer until you are sure what the question is. If it is not clear, restate it in your own words or ask the board member to clarify it for you. However, do not haggle about minor elements.

10) Reply promptly but not hastily

A common entry on oral board rating sheets is "candidate responded readily," or "candidate hesitated in replies." Respond as promptly and quickly as you can, but do not jump to a hasty, ill-considered answer.

11) Do not be peremptory in your answers

A brief answer is proper – but do not fire your answer back. That is a losing game from your point of view. The board member can probably ask questions much faster than you can answer them.

12) Do not try to create the answer you think the board member wants

He is interested in what kind of mind you have and how it works – not in playing games. Furthermore, he can usually spot this practice and will actually grade you down on it.

13) Do not switch sides in your reply merely to agree with a board member

Frequently, a member will take a contrary position merely to draw you out and to see if you are willing and able to defend your point of view. Do not start a debate, yet do not surrender a good position. If a position is worth taking, it is worth defending.

14) Do not be afraid to admit an error in judgment if you are shown to be wrong

The board knows that you are forced to reply without any opportunity for careful consideration. Your answer may be demonstrably wrong. If so, admit it and get on with the interview.

15) Do not dwell at length on your present job

The opening question may relate to your present assignment. Answer the question but do not go into an extended discussion. You are being examined for a *new* job, not your present one. As a matter of fact, try to phrase ALL your answers in terms of the job for which you are being examined.

Basis of Rating

Probably you will forget most of these "do's" and "don'ts" when you walk into the oral interview room. Even remembering them all will not ensure you a passing grade. Perhaps you did not have the qualifications in the first place. But remembering them will help you to put your best foot forward, without treading on the toes of the board members.

Rumor and popular opinion to the contrary notwithstanding, an oral board wants you to make the best appearance possible. They know you are under pressure – but they also want to see how you respond to it as a guide to what your reaction would be under the pressures of the job you seek. They will be influenced by the degree of poise you display, the personal traits you show and the manner in which you respond.

ABOUT THIS BOOK

This book contains tests divided into Examination Sections. Go through each test, answering every question in the margin. We have also attached a sample answer sheet at the back of the book that can be removed and used. At the end of each test look at the answer key and check your answers. On the ones you got wrong, look at the right answer choice and learn. Do not fill in the answers first. Do not memorize the questions and answers, but understand the answer and principles involved. On your test, the questions will likely be different from the samples. Questions are changed and new ones added. If you understand these past questions you should have success with any changes that arise. Tests may consist of several types of questions. We have additional books on each subject should more study be advisable or necessary for you. Finally, the more you study, the better prepared you will be. This book is intended to be the last thing you study before you walk into the examination room. Prior study of relevant texts is also recommended. NLC publishes some of these in our Fundamental Series. Knowledge and good sense are important factors in passing your exam. Good luck also helps. So now study this Passbook, absorb the material contained within and take that knowledge into the examination. Then do your best to pass that exam.

EXAMINATION SECTION

INTERVIEWING
EXAMINATION SECTION
TEST 1

DIRECTIONS: Each question or incomplete statement is followed by several suggested answers or completions. Select the one that BEST answers the question or completes the statement. *PRINT THE LETTER OF THE CORRECT ANSWER IN THE SPACE AT THE RIGHT.*

1. Of the following, the BEST way for an interviewer to calm a person who seems to have become emotionally upset as a result of a question asked is for the interviewer to

    A. talk to the person about other things for a short time
    B. ask that the person control himself
    C. probe for the cause of his emotional upset
    D. finish the questioning as quickly as possible

2. You find that an applicant is hesitant about showing you some required personal material and documents. Your *initial* reaction to this situation should be to

    A. quietly insist that he give you the required materials
    B. make an exception in his case to avoid making him uncomfortable
    C. suspect that he may be trying to withhold evidence
    D. understand that he is in a stressful situation and may feel ashamed to reveal such information

3. An applicant has just given you a response which does not seem clear.
   Of the following, the BEST course of action for you to take in order to check your understanding of the applicant's response is for you to

    A. ask the question again during a subsequent interview with this applicant
    B. repeat the applicant's answer in the applicant's own words and ask if that is what the applicant meant
    C. later in the interview, repeat the question that led to this response
    D. repeat the question that led to this response, but say it more forcefully

4. While speaking with applicants, you may find that there are times when an applicant will be silent for a short while before answering questions.
   In order to gather the best information from the applicant, the interviewer should *generally* treat these silences by

    A. repeating the same question to make the applicant stop hesitating
    B. rephrasing the question in a way that the applicant can answer it faster
    C. directing an easier question to the applicant so that he can gain confidence in answering
    D. waiting patiently and not pressuring the applicant into quick, undeveloped answers

5. In dealing with members of *different* ethnic and religious groups among the applicants you interview, you should give

    A. individuals the services to which they are entitled
    B. less service to those you judge to be more advantaged

C. better service to groups with which you sympathize most
D. better service to groups with political "muscle"

6. You must be sure that, when interviewing an applicant, you phrase each question carefully.
   Of the following, the MOST important reason for this is to insure that

   A. the applicant will phrase each of his responses carefully
   B. you use correct grammar
   C. it is clear to the applicant what information you are seeking
   D. you do not word the same question differently for different applicants

7. When given a form to complete, a client hesitates, tells you that he cannot fill out forms too well and that he is afraid he will do a poor job. He asks you to do it for him. You are quite sure, however, that he is able to do it himself.
   In this case, it would be MOST advisable for you to

   A. encourage him to try filling out the application as well as he can
   B. fill out the application for him
   C. explain to him that he must learn to accept responsibility
   D. tell him that, if others can fill out an application, he can too

8. Assume that an applicant whom you are interviewing has made a statement that is obviously not true.
   Of the following, the BEST course of action for you to take at this point in the interview is to

   A. ask the applicant if he is sure about his statement
   B. tell the applicant that his statement is incorrect
   C. question the applicant further to clarify his response
   D. assume that the statement is correct

9. Assume that you are conducting an *initial* interview with an applicant.
   Of the following, the MOST advisable questions for you to ask at the beginning of this interview are those that

   A. can be answered in one or two sentences
   B. have nothing to do with the subject matter of the interview
   C. are most likely to reveal any hostility on the part of the applicant
   D. the applicant is most likely to be willing and able to answer

10. When interviewing a particularly nervous and upset applicant, the one of the following actions which you should take FIRST is to

    A. inform the applicant that, to be helped, he must cooperate
    B. advise the applicant that proof must be provided for statements he makes
    C. assure the applicant that every effort will be made to provide him with whatever assistance he is entitled to
    D. tell the applicant he will have no trouble so long as he is truthful

11. Assume that it is part of your job to prepare a monthly report for your unit head that eventually goes to the director. The report contains information on the number of applicants you have interviewed that have been approved and the number of applicants you have interviewed that have been turned down. Errors on such reports are *serious* because

    A. you are expected to be able to prove how many applicants you have interviewed each month
    B. accurate statistics are needed for effective management of the department
    C. they may not be discovered before the report is transmitted to the director
    D. they may result in a loss to the applicants left out of the report

12. During interviews, people give information about themselves in several ways. Which of the following *usually* gives the LEAST amount of information about the person being questioned? His

    A. spoken words
    B. tone of voice
    C. facial expression
    D. body position

13. Suppose an applicant, while being interviewed, becomes angered by your questioning and begins to use sharp, uncontrolled language.
    Which of the following is the BEST way for you to react to him?

    A. Speak in his style to show him that you are neither impressed nor upset by his speech
    B. Interrupt him and tell him that you are not required to listen to this kind of speech
    C. Lower your voice and slow the rate of your speech in an attempt to set an example that will calm him
    D. Let him continue in his way but insist that he answer your questions directly

14. You have been informed that no determination has yet been made on the eligibility of an applicant whom you have interviewed. The decision depends on further checking. His situation, however, is similar to that of many other applicants whose eligibility has been approved. The applicant, *quite worried,* calls you, and asks whether his application has been accepted.
    What would be BEST for you to do under these circumstances? Tell him

    A. his application is being checked and you will let him know the final result as soon as possible
    B. that a written request addressed to your supervisor will probably get faster action for his case
    C. not to worry since other applicants with similar backgrounds have already been accepted
    D. since there is no definite information and you are very busy, you will call him back

15. Suppose that you have been talking with an applicant. You have the feeling from the latest things the applicant has said that some of his answers to earlier questions were not totally correct. You guess that he might have been afraid or confused earlier but that your conversation has now put him in a more comfortable frame of mind.
    In order to test the reliability of information received from the earlier questions, the BEST thing for you to do *now* is to ask new questions that

A. allow the applicant to explain why he deliberately gave false information to you
B. ask for the same information, although worded differently from the original questions
C. put pressure on the applicant so that he personally wants to clear up the facts in his earlier answers
D. indicate to the applicant that you are aware of his deceptiveness

16. While providing you with required information, an applicant whom you are interviewing, informs you that she does not know certain facts.
Of the following, the MOST advisable action for you to take is to

   A. ask her to explain further
   B. advise her about research facilities
   C. express your sympathy for the situation
   D. go on to the next item of information

17. If, in an interview, you wish to determine a client's usual occupation, which one of the following questions is MOST likely to elicit the *most* useful information?

   A. Did you ever work in a factory?
   B. Do you know how to do office work?
   C. What kind of work do you do?
   D. Where are you working now?

18. Assume that you are approached by a clerk from another office who starts questioning you about one of the clients you have just interviewed. The clerk says that she is a relative of the client. According to departmental policy, all matters discussed with clients are to be kept confidential.
Of the following, the BEST course of action for you to take in this situation would be to

   A. check to see whether the clerk is really a relative before you make any further decisions
   B. explain to the clerk why you cannot divulge the information
   C. tell the clerk that you do not know the answers to her questions
   D. tell the clerk that she can get from the client any information the client wishes to give

19. Which of the following is usually the BEST technique for you, as an interviewer, to use to bring an applicant back to subject matter from which the applicant has strayed?

   A. Ask the applicant a question that is related to the subject of the interview
   B. Show the applicant that his response is unrelated to the question
   C. Discreetly reind the applicant that there is a time allotment for the interview
   D. Tell the applicant that you will be happy to discuss the extraneous matters at a future interview

20. Assume that you are interviewing a witness who is telling a story crucial to your investigation. It is important that you get all the facts being related by this witness. In order to secure this vital information, the BEST of the following techniques is to

   A. quietly interrupt the witness's story and request him to speak with deliberation so that you can record his statement
   B. guide the witness during his recital so that all important points are validated

C. confine your activities during the story to brief note-taking, and, after the information has been secured, request a full written statement
D. inform the witness that he must relate all the facts as truthfully and concisely as possible

21. The statement of any witness obtained in an interview should GENERALLY be considered

    A. as a lead requiring substantiation by additional evidence
    B. accurate if the witness appears honest and is cooperative
    C. unreliable if the witness has been involved in similar investigations
    D. as a fact admissible under the rules of evidence

22. During an important interview, an interviewer takes notes from time to time but very rarely looks at the subject being questioned.
    Such action on the part of the interviewer is

    A. *unacceptable,* chiefly because during the actual interview an interviewer should pay more attention to the witness's manner of giving the information rather than to the content of his statements
    B. *acceptable,* chiefly because data should be recorded at the earliest opportunity and important data should be noted meticulously
    C. *unacceptable,* chiefly because it inhibits the person being interviewed and is not conducive to a give-and-take discussion
    D. *unacceptable,* chiefly because focusing attention on note-taking and not on the person being interviewed creates an impression of professional objectivity

23. Since he must interview persons with various personalities and attitudes, an interviewer should, *generally,* adopt a method of interviewing that

    A. is uniformly applicable to all types so that discrepancies in the accounts of individuals may be readily detected
    B. can be adjusted to the persons whom he interviews
    C. is based on the premise that most interviewees tend to be uncooperative
    D. requires the interviewer to spend as little time as possible in questioning applicants

24. One of the more difficult tasks facing an interviewer is to control the tendency of witnesses to ramble when giving information.
    Of the following, the BEST technique for keeping a witness's comments pertinent is to

    A. ask questions which indicate the desired answer
    B. insist on "yes" and "no" answers to his questions
    C. construct questions that restrict the range of information which the witness can give in response
    D. ask precise questions so that the answers of the witness will necessarily be brief

25. During interviews, a certain interviewer phrases follow-up questions mentally during pauses while the subject is still answering the previous question. This practice is, *generally,*

    A. *desirable,* chiefly because it gives the impression that the interviewer is well acquainted with all the facts
    B. *undesirable,* chiefly because the interviewer cannot know whether such questions will be appropriate
    C. *desirable,* chiefly because it enables the interviewer to pose new questions without significant breaks in the discussion
    D. *undesirable,* chiefly because it subjects the person being interviewed to a barrage of questions

---

KEY (CORRECT ANSWERS)

1.	A	11.	B
2.	D	12.	D
3.	B	13.	C
4.	D	14.	A
5.	A	15.	B
6.	C	16.	D
7.	A	17.	C
8.	C	18.	B
9.	D	19.	A
10.	C	20.	C

21.	A
22.	C
23.	B
24.	C
25.	C

TEST 2

DIRECTIONS: Each question or incomplete statement is followed by several suggested answers or completions. Select the one that BEST answers the question or completes the statement. *PRINT THE LETTER OF THE CORRECT ANSWER IN THE SPACE AT THE RIGHT.*

1. The one of the following which is the BEST description of a *properly* objective interviewer is one who

    A. is friendly and sensitive to the client's feelings, without becoming emotionally involved
    B. is distant and impersonal, remaining unaffected by what the client says
    C. lets personal emotions enter as far as the client's situation calls for them
    D. becomes emotionally involved with the client's situation, but without showing this involvement

    1.____

2. The one of the following which is MOST necessary for successfully interviewing a person who belongs to a culture different from that of the interviewer is for the interviewer to

    A. have some appreciation of the other culture
    B. ignore those cultural differences which lead to bias
    C. stay away from sensitive, "touchy" issues
    D. assume the mannerisms of people in the other culture

    2.____

3. In fact-finding interviews, it is generally assumed that the smaller the lumber of interviewees, the greater the increase of reliability with the addition of others.
The PROPER number of interviewees needed to insure the accuracy of information obtained *generally* depends upon the

    A. educational level of those interviewed
    B. number of people who have the required information
    C. directness of the questions asked
    D. variability of the information received

    3.____

4. The one of the following which is generally MOST likely to be *accurately* described in an interview by an interviewee is

    A. the presence of a large painting in the interviewer's office
    B. the number of people in the interviewer's waiting room
    C. space relations
    D. duration of time

    4.____

5. The one of the following which is *generally* the BEST course of action for an interviewer to take when interviewing a person who is reluctant to tell what he knows about a matter under investigation is to

    A. be curt and abrupt, and threaten the person with the consequences of his withholding information
    B. be firm and severe, and pressure the person into telling the needed information

    5.____

7

C. be patient and candid with the person being questioned about the investigation since doing otherwise is not ethical
D. give the person false information about the investigation so he will give the needed information without realizing its importance

6. It is often recommended that an interviewer prepare in advance a list of questions or topics to be covered in an interview.
The MAIN reason for using such a checklist is to

   A. allow investigations to be assigned to less efficient interviewers
   B. eliminate a large amount of follow-up paper work
   C. aid the interviewer in remembering to cover all important topics
   D. aid the interviewer in maintaining an objective distance from the person interviewed

7. *Usually*, the CHIEF advantage of a directive approach in an interview is that the

   A. interviewer maintains control over the course of the interview
   B. person interviewed is more likely to be put at ease
   C. person interviewed is generally left free to direct the interview
   D. interviewer will not suggest answers to the person interviewed

8. *Usually*, the CHIEF advantage of a non-directive approach in conducting an interview is that the

   A. interviewer generally conceals what he is looking for in the interview
   B. person interviewed is more likely to express his true feelings about the topic under discussion
   C. person interviewed is more likely to follow an idea introduced by the interviewer
   D. interviewer can keep the discussion limited to topics he believes to be relevant

9. The one of the following which is generally the LEAST likely to be *accurate* in a description of an event given to an interviewer is a statement about

   A. the presence of an object
   B. the number of people, when their number is small
   C. locations of people
   D. duration of time

10. Assume that you, an interviewer, are conducting a character investigation.
In an interview, the one of the following character traits of the person being interviewed which can *usually* be determined with a GOOD degree of reliability is

    A. honesty
    B. dependability
    C. forcefulness
    D. perseverance

11. You have been assigned the task of obtaining a family's social history.
The BEST place for you to interview members of the family while obtaining this social history would, *generally*, be in

    A. the family's home
    B. your agency's general offices
    C. the home of a friend of the family
    D. your own private office

12. If an interviewer obtains testimony from persons in interviews by means of interrogation or asking questions rather than by letting the person freely relate the testimony, what is said will, *generally*, be 12.____

    A. *greater* in range and *less* accurate
    B. *greater* in range and *more* accurate
    C. about the *same* in range and *less* accurate
    D. about the *same* in range and *more* accurate

13. Experienced interviewers have learned to phrase their questions carefully in order to obtain the desired response. Of the following, the question which would *usually* elicit the MOST accurate answer is: 13.____

    A. "How old are you?"
    B. "What is your income?"
    C. "How are you today?"
    D. "What is your date of birth?"

14. The one of the following questions which would *generally* lead to the LEAST reliable answer is: 14.____

    A. "Did you see a wallet?"
    B. "Was the German Shepherd gray?"
    C. "Didn't you see the stop sign?"
    D. "Did you see the guard on duty?"

15. Some interviewers may make a practice of observing details of the surroundings when interviewing in someone's home or office. 15.____
    Such a practice is, *generally*, considered

    A. *undesirable,* mainly because such snooping is an unwarranted, unethical invasion of privacy
    B. *undesirable,* mainly because useful information is rarely, if ever, gained this way
    C. *desirable,* mainly because useful insights into the character of the person interviewed may be gained
    D. *desirable,* mainly because it is impossible to evaluate a person adequately without such observation of his environment

KEY (CORRECT ANSWERS)

1. A	6. C	11. A
2. A	7. A	12. A
3. D	8. B	13. D
4. A	9. D	14. B
5. C	10. C	15. C

EXAMINATION SECTION
TEST 1

DIRECTIONS: Each question or incomplete statement is followed by several suggested answers or completions. Select the one that BEST answers the question or completes the statement. *PRINT THE LETTER OF THE CORRECT ANSWER IN THE SPACE AT THE RIGHT.*

1. The following three statements relate to master keys:
   I. The use of the apartment master key by project maintenance employees is authorized for emergencies which require widespread entrance to apartments
   II. Housing patrolmen receive apartment master keys but not maintenance master keys
   III. Defective or broken master keys must be sent to the Bay View Lock Shop only by registered mail.

   Which of the following choices lists all the foregoing statements that are generally CORRECT?

   A. I only is generally correct.
   B. II only is generally correct.
   C. III only is generally correct.
   D. I and III only are generally correct.

2. State legislation requires an owner, including the Authority, to install a bell, buzzer, and voice intercommunication system and to install self-closing and self-locking building entrance doors under certain conditions.
   The following three statements relate to such installations:
   I. The Authority is obligated to install such a system only when tenants occupying a majority of the apartments in a building make written request and agree to pay for the cost
   II. Tenants who do not request the installation need not pay for it
   III. Housing managers must meet with the executive committee of the tenant organization to discuss possible installation of the system.

   Which of the following choices list all the foregoing statements that are generally correct?

   A. I and II only are generally correct.
   B. II and III only are generally correct.
   C. I and III only are generally correct.
   D. I, II, and III are generally correct.

3. The following three statements relate to underoccupied apartments:
   I. A tenant may not be transferred to a smaller apartment unless he is eligible on the basis of income for the smaller apartment
   II. The Authority will pay moving expenses according to its schedule for a non-welfare tenant transferring to a smaller apartment
   III. When underoccupancy arises from death, no attempt to have the tenant move to a smaller apartment should be made for six months.

   Which of the following choices lists all the foregoing statements that are generally CORRECT?

A. I only is generally correct.
B. II only is generally correct.
C. I and II only are generally correct.
D. II and III only are generally correct.

4. The following three statements relate to the project operating budget:
    I. The second- and third-year figures of the three-year budget may be more of an estimate than those for the first year
    II. Housing managers may consult with technicians in the technical service division about budget matters
    III. Each housing manager and superintendent shall maintain a file to be known as *operating budget preparation folder*.
   Which of the following choices lists all the foregoing statements that are generally CORRECT?

    A. I and II only are generally correct.
    B. II and III only are generally correct.
    C. I and III only are generally correct.
    D. I, II, and III are generally correct.

5. The following three statements relate to apartment visits by housing assistants in subsidized projects:
    I. If there are indications of a problem situation or negligent use of the apartment, the housing assistant must visit all the rooms
    II. The tenant has the option of refusing both the orientation visit made after move-in and the annual visit
    III. If there is no record of poor housekeeping, and at first glance the apartment appears to be in reasonably good order, the housing assistant should limit his inspection to the range and the refrigerator.
   Which of the following choices lists all the foregoing statements that are generally CORRECT?

    A. I only is generally correct.
    B. I and II only are generally correct.
    C. II only is generally correct.
    D. II and III only are generally correct.

6. The following three statements relate to the use of project space for community purposes:
    I. All groups requesting space must first apply to the housing manager
    II. The housing manager must notify the legal department immediately upon the vacating of community space by the lessee or upon a major change in the use of space.
    III. The housing manager must maintain a ledger card for each community space under lease and collect rent for such space.
   Which of the following choices lists all the foregoing statements that are generally CORRECT?

    A. I, II, and III are generally correct.
    B. I and II only are generally correct.
    C. II and III only are generally correct.
    D. I and III only are generally correct.

3 (#1)

7. A newspaper reporter calls to interview you about a fire that occurred the previous evening in a tenant's apartment. All their furnishings and clothing were destroyed either through fire or water damage. The family was forced to spend the night with several neighbors. You have been authorized to grant the interview.
Which of the following statements would be PROPER for you to make?
The family

   A. has been a problem to management because of poor apartment maintenance
   B. is being moved to a smaller apartment in the project because they are destitute
   C. is being relocated to another apartment because of complaints from neighbors
   D. is being moved into a vacant apartment, since it will take some days to rehabilitate their apartment

7._____

8. A press photographer requests permission to take pictures from the roof of a high-rise building. The housing manager at the project should

   A. reject the request in order to comply with the regulations
   B. reject the request because the Authority has no third-party insurance
   C. check his credentials and request permission from the public relations office
   D. verify his credentials and allow him to photograph from the roof

8._____

9. Assume that the tenant patrol has been very effective in a high-rise building in reducing crime and vandalism. However, an incident involving an argument between two youths brings a crowd to the lobby. A patrol volunteer in the lobby has supported the Puerto Rican boy involved, whereas the tenants congregated support the Chinese boy involved. The police are called to disperse the crowd. Later you receive complaints that the patrol in the lobby mistreats the Chinese boys. The incident seems to have stirred up unrest throughout the building.
Of the following, the BEST way to handle this problem would be to

   A. investigate the charges and, if verified, disband the patrol
   B. request assistance from the office of community affairs at central office
   C. call in the parents and the boys involved in the incident and discuss continued occupancy reevalua-tions
   D. advise the complaining tenants that the patrol is dedicated to their security

9._____

10. Assume that tenant patrol volunteers in one of your 16 buildings request permission to store their lobby table and chairs in the electric meter room. Unless they can store their equipment, they will give up the work, since none of them is willing to continue cluttering his apartment with this equipment.
You should reject this request and attempt to find another remedy because

   A. buildings serviced by other patrols do not have similar storage space
   B. you doubt that proper room security can be permanently provided
   C. there might be a temptation to store items other than tables and chairs
   D. it is unlawful to use electric meter rooms for storage

10._____

11. A recommendation to terminate tenancy may be made because of alcoholism where it results in

   A. related medical conditions of a chronic nature
   B. family estrangement leading to divorce proceedings

11._____

13

C. interference with the proper operations of the project
D. substantial reduction in total family income

12. A guide to tenants furnished by a project may NOT give information concerning the address of the local

    A. medicaid alert office
    B. city hospital
    C. Department of Health clinic
    D. drugstore

13. From time to time, employees have been accused of improper actions or behavior while working in apartments. Therefore, when there is someone in the apartment, it is important that certain rules of conduct be observed.
    The one of the following which is NOT such a rule is for employees to

    A. place the official *door knob notice* on the door on entering an apartment
    B. avoid any discussion with children
    C. leave the apartment if anyone appears to be under the influence of liquor
    D. discuss the reason for leaving the door open while working

14. The CHIEF function of the housing manager in dealing with a tenants' association is to

    A. listen to their requests and to advise them on Authority policies
    B. provide leadership in conducting their affairs
    C. attend meetings solely to report their activities to the chief manager
    D. attend meetings to identify certain undesirable militants

15. Certain tenants may keep animals within certain limitations.
    The one of the following which is NOT a specific category of such tenants is

    A. mute
    B. blind
    C. elderly
    D. severely handicapped

16. The project office is being picketed by a number of tenants protesting a recent Authority-wide rent increase. The one of the following that the housing manager is LEAST likely to notify is the

    A. public information division
    B. office of the chief of the administration division
    C. chief manager
    D. department of social and community services

17. As manager of a site clearance project, you learn that a tenant of record had just vacated, leaving in possession persons who have been in occupancy for more than six months.
    Consistent with the policy on sharing families, you should

    A. consider the remaining persons as tenants
    B. institute summary holdover proceedings
    C. request a notarized certificate of necessity from the occupants
    D. refer the matter to the legal department for disposition

18. On a site you manage, a residential tenant on firm rent refuses to pay the approved scheduled rent.
Of the following actions, the one you should take IMMEDIATELY is to

   A. determine whether a rent reduction is justified
   B. institute summary proceedings for non-payment
   C. notify the tenant of the commencement of the one-month penalty period
   D. refer the matter to the chief of site management

19. Referral of the tenant to the social services division is advisable in all of the following situations EXCEPT that of a(n)

   A. elderly tenant disturbing her neighbors by irrational behavior
   B. young mother separated from her husband complaining that her worker is not responsive to her needs
   C. tenant admitting that she cannot control the disruptive behavior of her ten-year-old twins
   D. young mother separated from her husband being the subject of frequent complaints by several neighbors in reference to unreasonably noisy parties

20. Submission of a tenant's record to the office of the tenancy administrator for termination review is mandatory when a

   A. tenant's son is arrested for selling narcotics off-project
   B. tenant is arrested for assaulting his wife with his fists
   C. tenant's brother is arrested for possession of marijuana in a neighborhood youth center
   D. tenant is arrested for forgery of his sister's signature

21. A housing police patrolman requests supper money because he worked a tour of 8:00 M. to 8:00 P.M. The overtime was a result of his arresting a suspect caught leaving an apartment with the tenant's television set.
You are obliged to REJECT the request because

   A. the housing police are not granted supper money in any circumstances
   B. the management petty cash funds cannot be used for police work
   C. the officer was off duty at 8:00 P.M., and it was unreasonable to expect supper money
   D. only his sergeant may authorize such supper money

22. The housing police have submitted an incident report to you involving a tenant of a neighboring project. It is a minor incident which took place in your project and which also involved several of your tenants.
Of the following actions, you are REQUIRED to

   A. request an interview with the non-tenant at his convenience
   B. write a letter to the non-tenant warning of penalties if the incident recurs
   C. notify the other manager and send a copy of the incident report
   D. arrange with the other manager for a joint conference

23. The housing police apprehend a 12-year-old boy, living in the project, chipping away at the elevator buttons in the lobby and defacing the wall tiles. The damage is thereafter repaired at a cost of $75. The responsible tenant refuses to pay for this damage.
In order to recover the expense of this unlawful destruction, the housing manager may

    A. institute a civil damage suit in small claims court
    B. ask the chief manager to evaluate whether a civil damage suit should be brought
    C. include the charge in a dispossession for non-payment of rent
    D. refer the responsible tenant to the social services division for consultation

24. Assume that the housing police advise you that a tenant has been found murdered in his apartment.
The FIRST action you should take is to

    A. call the local police precinct
    B. notify the president of the tenants' association
    C. call the public relations division
    D. notify the legal division

25. Data show a relationship between felony rates in housing projects and certain other factors. This data showed that, in projects with well-structured moderate-income families, the felony rate per 1,000 families

    A. *falls* as the density of dwelling units per acre increases
    B. *rises* as the density of dwelling units per acre decreases
    C. *falls* as the height of buildings increases
    D. *rises* as the height of buildings increases

KEY (CORRECT ANSWERS)

1.	A	11.	C
2.	C	12.	D
3.	B	13.	D
4.	D	14.	A
5.	A	15.	C
6.	D	16.	D
7.	D	17.	A
8.	C	18.	B
9.	B	19.	B
10.	D	20.	A

21. A
22. C
23. B
24. C
25. D

TEST 2

DIRECTIONS: Each question or incomplete statement is followed by several suggested answers or completions. Select the one that BEST answers the question or completes the statement. *PRINT THE LETTER OF THE CORRECT ANSWER IN THE SPACE AT THE RIGHT.*

1. Assume that a housing manager of a large subsidized project advised her senior teller to have the petty cash fund available for inspection on the afternoon of the third Wednesday of the month.
   This practice is considered to be

   A. *desirable* because such an inspection will not interfere with the bookkeeping office when rent is being collected
   B. *undesirable* because an audit of the petty cash fund should be unannounced
   C. *desirable* because it will encourage a better relationship between the manager and the teller
   D. *undesirable* because the third Wednesday may be a welfare check day

   1.____

2. The Authority carries insurance policies for indemnification against certain losses or damages.
   The one of the following for which the Authority is NOT insured is

   A. damage caused by a strike
   B. claims by persons other than employees, including damages for care and loss of services
   C. coverage for alteration of any check, draft, or promissory note
   D. protection against claims by tenants for damage to personal property by employees

   2.____

3. Assume that, as housing manager, you are presented with contract papers which require your signature before payment can be made. The papers are for partial payment for roofing work at a total cost of $50,000. The superintendent and the plant services inspector have already signed, indicating that work has been satisfactorily completed to date.
   Of the following, the BEST reason for you to sign the papers is that

   A. the signatures of the superintendent and the inspector assure that payment is in order
   B. the superintendent has requested you to sign the papers immediately to insure prompt payment
   C. you are satisfied that the work to date complies with the contract
   D. the rules of the Authority requires that the manager sign that he is aware of the progress of the work

   3.____

4. You have posted on the bulletin board in the bookkeeping office information issued by the Treasury Department giving descriptions of counterfeit $20 bills in circulation. The branch bank handling the project account advises you that the previous night's deposit contained a counterfeit $20 bill.
   The one of the following actions you should take is to

   A. request the cashier who accepted the bill to make restitution
   B. request the cashier who accepted the bill to process a shortage adjustment report and sign it

   4.____

17

C. call the U.S. Treasury Department to report the matter
D. call the housing police for assistance in tracing the passer

5. An aged tenant of the project requests that the teller cash a city payroll check for $287.50 made out to his wife. The check bears the wife's endorsement and the tenant endorses the check in front of the teller. He does not wish to pay his rent at this time. The teller cashes the check.
The teller's action is

   A. *correct;* city payroll checks in any amount should be cashed for tenants
   B. *correct*; this tenant was entitled to have this check cashed
   C. *incorrect;* the tenant should have presented his wife's authorization on a consent to second-party payee form
   D. *incorrect;* the check was payable only to the tenant's spouse

6. Assume that, at the project, a stalled elevator is brought down to floor level. None of the passengers has suffered injury, appear to be in shock or request medical attention. They leave the elevator in a normal manner. One of the passengers is carrying a sleeping infant in her arms.
In this situation, you should GENERALLY

   A. refer adult passengers to the legal department
   B. refrain from submitting a report of the incident
   C. submit a report of accident, public liability
   D. telephone the insurance adjuster for specific instructions

7. A charge may PROPERLY be imposed on tenants for

   A. certain instances of repainting
   B. minor repairs when a tenant is vacating
   C. a transfer to an apartment of a different size to conform to occupancy standards
   D. repair of two leaking faucets

8. A project audit by the audit section of the control department reveals a large number of discrepancies between the E.D.P. listings of tools, equipment, and material and the physical inventory.
Of the following, the LEAST desirable action to take in this situation is to

   A. review all procedures relating to issuing tools and withdrawals from the storeroom
   B. call the housing police detective squad to investigate
   C. institute a semi-annual internal audit covering all accountable items
   D. review storage security

9. The one of the following which is CONSISTENT with the policies and procedures for prevention and elimination of pest and rodent infestation is that

   A. all vacated apartments should be treated for roach infestation
   B. the foreman of pest control operators must inspect the personal property of all intra-project transfer tenants for infestation
   C. in cases of serious infestation the tenant may be required to empty all closets
   D. if no infestation is found in a routine inspection, the premises are not treated

10. You have learned that the maintenance men refuse to make a repair in an apartment because of what they consider filthy housekeeping.
    Of the following actions, the one which would be BEST for you to take FIRST is to

    A. write a letter to the tenant explaining the reason the repair has not been made
    B. send a work order to the superintendent, asking that it be returned showing when the work was completed
    C. inform the superintendent of the situation, and advise him of management's responsibility to make the repair
    D. direct the maintenance men to follow up on the housekeeping problem to insure compliance before the work is done

11. Tenants who wish to install their own refrigerators in place of refrigerators provided by the Authority may do so subject to certain regulation.
    The one of the following statements which is such a regulation is that

    A. requests for installation of tenant-owned refrigerators must be submitted to the superintendent for approval
    B. refrigerators with dual temperature controls are not permitted
    C. only extension cords bearing U.L. approval may be used between refrigerators and wall outlets
    D. tenant-owned refrigerators may be installed only in kitchens

12. A tenant complains to you that the painter shattered a $50 mirror. The tenant requests payment for the mirror. The painter is an employee of the contractor and not of the Authority.
    The one of the following actions that you should take in handling this complaint is to

    A. approve a property damage claim for 90% of the loss
    B. refer the tenant to the contractor to whom she should present her claim
    C. advise the contractor of the claim and request that the tenant be paid
    D. prepare and submit to the legal department a notice of claim

13. In the event of fire in the boiler plant, the FIRST step to take is to

    A. fight the fire with the prescribed fire extinguisher
    B. ask the first person passing by to call the Fire Department
    C. activate the nearest Fire Department alarm box
    D. pull the remote control switch

14. Assume that a boiler explosion has occurred. The resulting damage is less than $700.
    Of the following actions, the one which the manager should take FIRST is to

    A. consult with the chief of insurance
    B. proceed through the superintendent to repair or restore the premises
    C. request a performance bond from a designated outside contractor
    D. report the problem to the state division of housing and community renewal

15. Top priority in snow removal must be given to

    A. clearing ramps and interior secondary sidewalks
    B. providing access to fuel lines and fire hydrants
    C. building entrance steps and entrance landings
    D. interior sidewalks leading from buildings directly to perimeter sidewalks

16. A housing manager may approve a request for an inter-project transfer when the tenant
    A. who is the principal wage-earner was transferred two months ago to a new work location requiring two hours' traveling time
    B. who has a chronic illness or a physical handicap requires specialized care or facilities not available near the project
    C. is in an overcrowded apartment because a daughter who was an original member of the family has returned home with her husband
    D. in a middle-income project requests a transfer to a subsidized project because he has been on strike for two months

17. The assistant housing manager requests your advice, as housing manager, about an unauthorized occupancy. A daughter and her two children have moved into a tenant's apartment. The tenant family consists of husband, wife, and teenage son. The tenant is receiving aid from the department of social services and produces evidence that the three additional family members have also been budgeted since their unauthorized move-in about a year ago. Therefore, the tenant should be advised
    A. to seek special permission from the housing consultant for this occupancy arrangement
    B. to tell the three additional occupants to move out and then apply for approval to move into this apartment
    C. that since there has been no change in rent you will approve a change in status
    D. that the Authority considers the family composition to be in violation of occupancy standards

18. Assume that in the course of a regular call to an apartment by an employee a serious quarrel arises among several adults who are in the apartment.
    Of the following, the MOST important rule for the employee to follow is to
    A. observe these persons carefully to determine possible signs of intoxication or of substance abuse
    B. attempt to mediate the dispute so that he may proceed to complete his assigned tasks without interruption
    C. instruct the tenants and their guests, if any, as to their privileges and responsibilities relative to the premises
    D. avoid involvement and, if necessary, leave the apartment

19. For a residual single person to remain in occupancy, he is required to
    A. have reached age 30
    B. be ambulatory
    C. accept immediate transfer to a smaller apartment
    D. pass a monthly apartment inspection for six consecutive months

20. You have evicted a tenant whose entire furnishings have been placed on the street on the order of the marshal, who has given you possession of the apartment.
    Of the following, it would be CORRECT for you to
    A. have the department of sanitation dispose of the street encumbrance
    B. have project personnel dispose of the encumbrance by commercial storage
    C. charge the tenant's account for the cost of removing the encumbrance
    D. charge the tenant on a time basis for removal from the street by project staff

21. Assume that you have decided to recommend termination of tenancy based on non-desirability.
    The way in which you should treat the facts or incidents and their sources upon which you relied for your decision should be to

    A. *withhold* the facts, although the source may be revealed to the tenant
    B. *reveal* the facts, although the source need not be revealed to the tenant
    C. *reveal* the facts and the source to the tenant
    D. *withhold* the facts and the source from the tenant

21._____

22. A single elderly occupant is found dead in his apartment. You have been unable to locate any relatives or references appearing in the tenant record, despite diligent efforts.
    You may, therefore, take possession of the apartment ONLY if

    A. you receive a release from the public administrator's office
    B. there is more than one month's rent in arrears
    C. the furnishings are considered worthless
    D. the police find the keys in the apartment and turn them over to you

22._____

23. When a manager decides that a tenant's shades are in such condition that replacement is required, and he provides the tenant with used shades, there shall be _____ charge.

    A. a charge of 3/4 of the scheduled
    B. a charge of 1/2 of the scheduled
    C. a charge of 1/4 of the scheduled
    D. no

23._____

24. Certain public agencies are entitled to full disclosure of confidential information concerning tenants or applicants.
    One such agency is the State

    A. Crime Victims Compensation Board
    B. Department of Audit and Control
    C. Division of Housing and Community Renewal
    D. Division of Municipal Affairs

24._____

25. Assume that you are asked by a local community organization to serve on a special committee which is to select an executive director for the organization. You accept the invitation and subsequently interview several candidates.
    Which of the following is the LEAST important consideration in reaching a valid decision about the suitability of each candidate for the position?

    A. Amount and sequence of experience in the candidate's work history
    B. Candidate's behavior during the interview
    C. Inferences concerning the candidate's underlying motives for seeking the position
    D. General qualifications needed for satisfactory job performance by a candidate

25._____

KEY (CORRECT ANSWERS)

1.	B	11.	D
2.	A	12.	B
3.	C	13.	D
4.	B	14.	B
5.	B	15.	B
6.	B	16.	B
7.	A	17.	D
8.	B	18.	D
9.	C	19.	B
10.	C	20.	C

21. B
22. A
23. D
24. C
25. C

TEST 3

DIRECTIONS: Each question or incomplete statement is followed by several suggested answers or completions. Select the one that BEST answers the question or completes the statement. *PRINT THE LETTER OF THE CORRECT ANSWER IN THE SPACE AT THE RIGHT.*

1. Authority officials have stressed that crime reported in public housing is proportionately much less than crime reported in the city as a whole. Some critics, however, hold such a comparison to mean little.
   Which of the following statements BEST supports the view of these critics?

   A. In compiling its data, the Authority uses a method different from the uniform crime reporting system of the city's Police Department.
   B. Many crime victims do not report crimes because they fear retaliation by criminals or believe that the police can do nothing.
   C. Recent sharp drops in reported crime have resulted from a temporary increase in security measures in the project.
   D. There are generally more commercial establishments and other inviting targets for criminals outside, rather than inside, housing projects.

   1._____

2. The Authority police consider a major impediment to the performance of their duties to be an unacceptably large number of defects in

   A. locks   B. radios
   C. handcuffs   D. ammunition

   2._____

3. MOST disagreements between the Authority police and the city police are caused by

   A. differences in salaries
   B. jurisdictional disputes
   C. conflicts concerning peace officer and police officer status
   D. unequal advancement opportunities

   3._____

4. Designated employee union representatives are permitted to be released with pay by the housing manager for several purposes.
   For which of the following activities would released time be WITHOUT pay?

   A. Investigation of grievances
   B. Participating in meetings of departmental joint labor relations committees
   C. Negotiating with and appearing before departmental and other city officials and agencies
   D. Attendance at union meetings or conventions

   4._____

5. Assume that you are the trial officer in a local disciplinary trial of a maintenance man based on charges by the superintendent that he demanded $2.00 from each tenant for whom he had installed a door-lock chain provided by the tenant. At the hearing, it develops that much more serious wrongdoing appears to have occurred.
   As trial officer, you believe that maximum penalties available to you are inadequate in this case. Of the following action, it would be MOST appropriate for you to

   A. advise the maintenance man to seek competent counsel
   B. impose a separate maximum penalty for each instance of wrongdoing

   5._____

C. postpone the trial and present the information to the District Attorney
D. suspend the trial and consult with the Authority's general counsel

6. Monthly toll telephone charges reveal a number of costly personal calls in the sum of $50 traced to an employee. Despite the evidence, the employee denies the accusation and refuses to pay the charges. You decide to hold a local disciplinary hearing.
The one of the following actions you are REQUIRED to take is to

   A. discuss the problem with the chief manager before taking any other action
   B. advise the employee you will be the hearing officer
   C. give the employée a notice of disciplinary charges indicating the charges and time and place of hearing
   D. advise the employee that the technical rules of evidence will be adhered to at the hearing

7. The housing manager has authority to write off claims in favor of or against the Authority within specified amounts. In accordance with this policy, the housing manager may

   A. dispose of any claim by a tenant or former tenant provided the amount of the payment does not exceed $50
   B. dispose of any claim by a tenant or former tenant provided the amount of the payment does not exceed $25
   C. write off any claim against a tenant in residence if the amount does not exceed $25
   D. write off any claim against a former tenant if the amount does not exceed $75

8. The one of the following statements which is CORRECT in reference to assets and eligibility for continued occupancy is that

   A. any tenant whose assets exceed three times the continued occupancy limit for his size apartment is ineligible
   B. a tenant who owns a building which contains a suitable dwelling unit in which he can live is ineligible if his equity in the building exceeds three times the occupancy limit
   C. a tenant whose earning capacity is limited or nonexistent is exempted from any limitation on excess assets for eligibility for continued occupancy provided that the district chief manager approves such exemption
   D. assets are defined to include cash on hand and in banks and the initial purchase value of real property, stocks, and bonds, and other forms of capital investment

9. Families determined as falling within certain categories may be declared ineligible for admission to public housing projects in the absence of extenuating circumstances. The one of the following which is SUCH a category is a family in which a(n)

   A. member of the family was involved in the sale of narcotics more than five years before the rental interview
   B. member of the family is a confirmed addict and is not undergoing follow-up treatment by a professional agency after discharge from an institution
   C. member of the family under the age of sixteen was involved as an offender in a crime of a sexual nature such as rape, carnal abuse, or impairing the morals of a minor
   D. adult member of the family was involved in an act of violence not of a serious criminal nature

10. The TOTAL proportion of apartments painted which the housing manager and the superintendent should inspect, or have inspected, is usually about

    A. 10%   B. 20%   C. 30%   D. 40%

11. Because of the great demand for housing in the city, some developments have been constructed on landfill on reclaimed river edges.
    One such project is

    A. Roosevelt Island
    B. Brooklyn Bridge Southwest
    C. Battery Park City
    D. Twin Parks

12. The issue raised by the plaintiffs in the recent legal suit against the Authority regarding the public housing in the Seward Park Extension Urban Renewal Area was the granting of preference in tenant selection to

    A. large families
    B. families from outside the area
    C. families of war veterans
    D. non-welfare families

13. *Exclusionary zoning* leads to residential segregation by social class or race.
    The one of the following MOST likely to lead to exclusionary zoning is for a state to permit

    A. apartment units to be of various sizes
    B. low-income housing to be built on private land
    C. municipalities to control building permits
    D. unrelated persons to live together

14. The portion of the Administrative Code that sets minimum standards for decent, safe, and sanitary dwellings is known as the _____ Code.

    A. General Construction   B. Multiple Dwelling
    C. Housing Maintenance   D. Building Standards

15. Of the following, which is the MOST accurate general description of the book, DEFENSIBLE SPACE, by Oscar Newman?
    The book

    A. is a detailed study of the architectural design of public housing projects in the city for the purpose of achieving greater economy of materials
    B. advocates using architectural design to create an environment for the enhancement of inhabitants' lives while also providing security for their families, neighbors, and friends
    C. concludes that a large police force is the major protection against most ordinary kinds of crime in public housing
    D. proposes high-rise developments as the rational remedy for chronic housing shortages and the most effective use of urban space

16. In recent years, a number of cities have emphasized the construction of low-rise vest-pocket public housing projects.
The one of the following which is the MAJOR disadvantage of this type of public housing, compared to larger-scale public housing projects, is that it

   A. has relatively higher tenant-borne operating and maintenance costs
   B. is more likely to encourage criminal activity
   C. inhibits community activities among tenants
   D. must be located at considerable distance from the central city

17. The one of the following which is usually LEAST significant in predicting whether a particular building located in a disadvantaged area of the city will be abandoned is

   A. its condition in comparison to low-income housing in other parts of the city
   B. the cost of maintaining it in good repair
   C. the extent of the drug addiction problem and criminal activity in the immediate neighborhood
   D. the attitude and behavior of the tenants of the particular building

18. The one of the following which is the MOST important cause of the low vacancy rate in public housing in the city in comparison to vacancy rates in other cities is the

   A. similarity in architectural design between public housing and middle-income housing in the city
   B. stringent enforcement in the city of relevant housing codes
   C. greater proximity of public housing in the city to unskilled job markets
   D. relatively large number of households in the city public housing which consist of the working poor

19. Housing experts who advocate the construction of public housing, rental supplements, and similar direct subsidies usually attribute the shortage of adequate housing for low-income families PRIMARILY to

   A. racial discrimination which has resulted in a destructive attitude toward housing on the part of minority group members
   B. the absence of mass production techniques in the building industry
   C. the recurrent lack of mortgage credit
   D. the ability of major cities to mount effective housing programs

20. A federally-funded program of free legal service, serving persons with poverty-level income, represents many residents of public housing.
In the city, the program is known as

   A. the Bar Association of the City
   B. the Council Against Poverty
   C. Community Action for Legal Services
   D. the Community Service Society

21. The federal government has recently proposed reducing the rent of newly constructed subsidized units for low-income households and, instead, assisting such households through cash housing allowances.
This proposed program lacks a provision to

A. give low-income persons freedom to choose where and how to live
B. pay the difference between what low-income persons can afford and the fair rent value of the quarters
C. prohibit landlords from raising rents unduly
D. provide special grants for cities with low vacancy rates

22. The Federal housing policies of the 1960s were LEAST successful in

A. generating increased housing production
B. improving conditions in deteriorating neighborhoods
C. promoting economic stabilization of the housing industry
D. encouraging home ownership for moderate-income households

23. The following sentences, when put in correct order, constitute a complete paragraph. Select from among the choices listed below, the one in which the CORRECT order is shown.
    I. Project residents had first claim to this use, followed by surrounding neighborhood children.
    II. By contrast, recreation space within the project's interior was found to be used more often by both groups.
    III. Studies of the use of project grounds in many cities showed grounds left open for public use were neglected and unused, both by residents and by members of the surrounding community.
    IV. Project residents had clearly laid claim to the play spaces, setting up and enforcing unwritten rules for use.
    V. Each group, by experience, found their activities easily disrupted by other groups, and their claim to the use of space for recreation difficult to enforce.

The CORRECT answer is:

A. IV, V, I, II, III
B. V, II, IV, III, I
C. I, IV, III, II, V
D. III, V, II, IV, I

24. The following sentences, when put in correct order, constitute a complete paragraph. Select from among the choices listed below the one in which the CORRECT order is shown.
    I. They do not consider the problems correctable within the existing subsidy formula and social policy of accepting all eligible applicants regardless of social behavior and life style.
    II. A recent survey, however, indicated that tenants believe these problems correctable by local housing authorities and management within the existing financial formula.
    III. Many of the problems and complaints concerning public housing management and design have created resentment between the tenant and the landlord.
    IV. This same survey indicated that administrators and managers do not agree with the tenants.

The CORRECT answer is:

A. II, I, III, IV
B. I, III, IV, II
C. III, II, IV, I
D. IV, II, I, III

25. The following sentences, when put in correct order, constitute a complete paragraph. Select from among the choices listed below the one in which the CORRECT order is shown.

   I. In single family residences, there is usually enough distance between tenants to prevent occupants from annoying one another.
   II. For example, a certain small percentage of tenant families has one or more members addicted to alcohol.
   III. While managers believe in the right of individuals to live as they choose, the manager becomes concerned when the pattern of living jeopardizes others' rights.
   IV. Still others turn night into day, staging lusty entertainments which carry on into the hours when most tenants are trying to sleep.
   V. In apartment buildings, however, tenants live so closely together that any misbehavior can result in unpleasant living conditions.
   VI. Other families engage in violent argument.

The CORRECT answer is:

A. III, II, V, IV, VI, I
B. I, V, II, VI, IV, III
C. II, V, IV, I, III, VI
D. IV, II, V, VI, III, I

KEY (CORRECT ANSWERS)

1. D
2. B
3. B
4. D
5. D

6. C
7. B
8. C
9. B
10. B

11. C
12. B
13. C
14. C
15. B

16. A
17. A
18. D
19. C
20. C

21. C
22. B
23. D
24. C
25. B

EXAMINATION SECTION
TEST 1

DIRECTIONS: Each question or incomplete statement is followed by several suggested answers or completions. Select the one that BEST answers the question or completes the statement. *PRINT THE LETTER OF THE CORRECT ANSWER IN THE SPACE AT THE RIGHT.*

1. While interviewing tenants, an assistant should use the technique of interruption, beginning to speak when a tenant has temporarily paused at the end of a phrase or sentence, in order to

    A. limit the tenant's ability to voice his objection or complaints
    B. shorten, terminate, or redirect a tenant's response
    C. assert authority when he feels that the tenant is too conceited
    D. demonstrate to the tenant that pauses in speech should be avoided

2. An assistant might gain background information about a tenant by being aware of the person's speech during an interview.
Which one of the following patterns of speech would offer the LEAST accurate information about a tenant?
The

    A. number of slang expressions and the level of vocabulary
    B. presence and degree of an accent
    C. rate of speech and the audibility level
    D. presence of a physical speech defect

3. Suppose that you are interviewing a distressed tenant who claims that he was just laid off from his job and has no money to pay his rent.
Your FIRST action should be to

    A. ask if he has sought other employment or has other sources of income
    B. express your sympathy but explain that he must pay the rent on time
    C. inquire about the reasons he was laid off from work
    D. try to transfer him to a smaller apartment which he can afford

4. Suppose you have some background information on an applicant whom you are interviewing. During the interview, it appears that the applicant is giving you false information.
The BEST thing for you to do at that point is to

    A. pretend that you are not aware of the written facts and let him continue
    B. tell him what you already know and discuss the discrepancies with him
    C. terminate the interview and make a note that the applicant is untrustworthy
    D. tell him that because he is making false statements, he will not be eligible for an appointment

5. Since at present there are not many Spanish-speaking assistants, a Spanish-speaking applicant may want to bring his bilingual child with him to an interview to act as an interpreter.
Which of the following would be LEAST likely to affect the value of an interview in which an applicant's child has acted as interpreter?

1.____

2.____

3.____

4.____

5.____

A. It may make it undesirable for the assistant to ask certain questions.
B. A child may do an inadequate job of interpretation.
C. A child's answers may indicate his feelings toward his parents.
D. The applicant may not want to reveal all information in front of his child.

6. While you are showing families around a new project which will be ready for occupancy in a month, you are asked many questions concerning the present state of disorder in the halls and grounds of the buildings. These families are concerned that this condition will exist when they move in.
Of the following, the BEST way to handle this situation would be for you to

    A. assure the tenants that the buildings will all be clean and tidy when they are due to move in
    B. explain that almost everything will be completed when the tenants move in, but that temporary inconveniences tend to exist when one moves into a new project
    C. avoid answering the questions since the condition will exist, but emphasize the advantage of moving into a new project
    D. explain that because this is a low-income project, efficiency is reduced and it will, therefore, take more time to get the building ready

7. Assume that you are responsible for making apartment inspections.
To make a practice of setting up appointments with tenants before visiting is

    A. *good,* mainly because it allows the tenant time to become acquainted with household safety procedures
    B. *good,* mainly because it is demeaning and disrespectful of tenant's privacy to appear at the apartment unannounced
    C. *poor,* mainly because it will give the tenant an opportunity to clean the house, thus not giving a picture of normal conditions
    D. *poor,* mainly because tenants should be available at all times for inspections

8. Assume that you are approached by a tenant who seeks your help in dealing with her 12-year-old son, Joe. He apparently leaves for school each morning, but another child has just informed her that Joe has not been in school for a month. She is very upset and does not know what action to take.
The one of the following actions which you should recommend that she take as a FIRST step is to

    A. report the truancy to the school immediately so they can take action
    B. discuss the situation with Joe, inquiring as to the truth of the matter
    C. reprimand Joe or deprive him of something he wants to get him to go to school
    D. tell Joe to report to you to discuss an important matter

9. Suppose you have been informed by your supervisor that he has checked the applications that you have submitted and he found that you have categorized a disproportionate number of minority applicants as ineligible. You feel that you have impartially evaluated all of the applications.
Of the following, the MOST appropriate action for you to take is to

    A. request that he review the application forms with you to discuss the eligibility of specific applications
    B. tell him that you will look over the applications and change them to eligible

C. tell him that you will try to be more careful in the future when interviewing and qualifying applicants
D. provide as much evidence as possible showing your good treatment of members of minority groups in other situations

10. Suppose you have placed in an apartment a family that has recently arrived from a distant country. Other tenants have mentioned to you that they are puzzled by the new tenants' strange culture and wonder when they will adapt to our society.
Of the following, which aspect of their culture is MOST conducive to change?

   A. Religious beliefs
   B. Parent-child relationships
   C. Use of household appliances
   D. Customs observed at meal-time

11. Suppose a tenant, Mr. X, complains to you that the occupants of the apartment directly below his apartment play their boom box . very loudly, although he has repeatedly asked them to lower it.
Of the following, the BEST action for you to take is to

   A. suggest that Mr. X also play loud music in his apartment to show how annoying it can be
   B. inform Mr. X that there is nothing that you can do – Mr. X must deal with the tenants directly
   C. post a sign in the building lobby stating the Noise Abatement Laws
   D. speak with the other tenant and discuss the situation with him

12. Suppose one of your duties includes inspecting the apartments of all new tenants and suggesting proper care of equipment. A family you are visiting appears to be quite hostile to you, although you have explained the purpose of your visit. You notice that the stove is covered with grease and the sink drain is clogged with coffee grounds. Of the following, what is the BEST thing for you to do in this situation?

   A. Refrain from making comments on the situation at this time, but remember to report the conditions to your supervisor
   B. Describe the dangers or possible results of the clogged drain and greasy stove, and suggest easy ways to correct these conditions
   C. Offer to help clean the stove and sink drain and enumerate, on paper, the ways to take care of the equipment properly
   D. Make an appointment for the tenants to speak with you about the situation in your office

13. Assume you are assigned to interview applicants for low-rent apartments.
Of the following, which is the BEST attitude for you to take in dealing with applicants for apartments?

   A. Assume they will enjoy being interviewed because they believe that you, as a representative of the landlord, will get them an apartment
   B. Expect that they have had a history of anti-social behavior in the family, and probe deeply into the social development of family members
   C. Expect that they will try to control the interview, thus you should keep them on the defensive

D. Assume that they will be polite and cooperative and attempt to secure the information you need in a business-like manner

14. Assume that the following problem of a tenant family has come to your attention. The tenant, who is the main support of his family, has developed a health problem which prevents him from driving a car or traveling to work by subway. He can, however, walk up to a mile or travel by surface transportation. Because of the problem of traveling to work, he may lose his job.
Which of the following courses of action should you take FIRST?

    A. Put the tenant in touch with the department of social services. They may be able to arrange public assistance payments for him.
    B. Find out whether any housing projects meeting the new transportation restrictions of the tenant have any apartments available.
    C. Arrange a visit by a social worker. If the man stays home and his wife goes to work, they may be able to maintain their income.
    D. Send the man for employment counseling. He may have skills that are in demand, close to his present apartment.

15. Assume that an elderly single tenant who has habitually paid her rent on time is now two weeks late with her current month's rent. You have sent her an official notice of delinquency.
Assuming that you have taken no other action to collect the rent, the NEXT thing you should do is to

    A. send her a strong personal note demanding payment of her rent
    B. send a polite note to her daughter, who is listed on your records as next of kin, asking her to speak to her mother about her delinquency
    C. send her a note asking her to telephone you immediately
    D. telephone or visit her apartment because illness may be the cause of the late rent payment

16. Assume that you are working at a project and a tenant tells you that some equipment left on the grounds poses a hazard to the tenants and their children. She suggests that this equipment be surrounded by barricades and signs.
Of the following, the BEST response for you to make is to tell the tenant

    A. to route her complaint and suggestion through the tenants' association
    B. that you will pass her complaint and suggestion on to the manager of the project for consideration
    C. to be careful in making complaints; she may be labeled as a troublemaker
    D. suggest that she put her complaint and suggestion into writing so that it will be easier to understand

17. Assume that, in a public housing project, a tenant complains that the interior of the elevator has recently been defaced by graffiti. She claims that for the past two days, at about 3 P.M., she has seen a few teenage boys running from the building and suspects they are the culprits.
The FIRST thing that you should do is to

    A. station a housing patrolman by the elevator for the next few days to observe any unusual incidents
    B. explain to her that the incidents appear to be totally unrelated

C. have a housing patrolman patrol the outside of the building at 3 P.M. to watch for the boys
D. ask her why she feels the boys are responsible for the graffiti

Questions 18-20.

DIRECTIONS: Questions 18 through 20 each list various duties that you are to perform on a particular day. Assuming that you have arrived at the office at 9:00 A.M., indicate for each question which of the four duties listed should be taken care of FIRST.

18. A. You are informed that an elderly tenant has just been taken to the hospital and you must call his son, whose telephone number you have on file.
    B. Two tenants whose children have been involved in a series of complaints concerning damage to housing authority property are waiting to see you.
    C. You have a message from the central office of the housing authority requesting clarification of a single point in a report you prepared.
    D. A tenant who was already served with an eviction notice for non-payment of rent is waiting with a large back-rent check.

19. A. A tenant who is about to be evicted because of non-payment of rent is waiting to see you.
    B. A housing patrolman who must leave for court wants to speak to you about a tenant's child he has just arrested.
    C. It will take only ten minutes to finish your monthly activities report which is overdue.
    D. An insurance investigator is waiting to see you concerning an injury suffered by a tenant in his building's elevator.

20. A. The receptionist tells you that a woman is waiting to see you with a complaint about a repair to a toilet. The woman says she must leave for work by 9:30 A.M.
    B. You have an unfinished report in your desk which requires about 15 minutes to complete,
    C. A tenant is early for a 9:15 appointment for an interview that should take approximately 15 minutes.
    D. There is a note to you from the project manager which says, *Please see me as soon as you can spare 15 minutes.*

KEY (CORRECT ANSWERS)

1. B	6. B	11. D	16. B
2. C	7. B	12. B	17. D
3. A	8. B	13. D	18. A
4. B	9. A	14. B	19. B
5. C	10. C	15. D	20. A

TEST 2

DIRECTIONS: Each question or incomplete statement is followed by several suggested answers or completions. Select the one that BEST answers the question or completes the statement. *PRINT THE LETTER OF THE CORRECT ANSWER IN THE SPACE AT THE RIGHT.*

Questions 1-5.

DIRECTIONS: Questions 1 through 5 are to be answered SOLELY on the basis of the following passage.

At one time people thought that in the interview designed primarily to obtain information, the interviewer had to resort to clever and subtle lines of questioning in order to accomplish his ends. Some people still believe that this is necessary, but it is not so. An example of the "tricky" approach may be seen in the work of a recent study. The study deals with materials likely to be buried beneath deep defenses. Interviewers utilized methods of questioning which, in effect, trapped the interviewee and destroyed his defenses. Doubtless these methods succeeded in bringing out items of information which straightforward questions would have missed. Whether they missed more information than they obtained and whether they obtained the most important facts must remain unanswered questions. In defense of the "clever" approach, it is often said that, in many situations, the interviewee is motivated to conceal information or to distort what he chooses to report.

Technically, it is likely that a highly skilled interviewer can, given the time and the inclination, penetrate the interviewee's defenses and get information which the latter intended to keep hidden. It is unlikely that the interviewer can successfully elicit all of the information that might be relevant. If, for example, he found that an applicant for financial assistance was heavily in debt to gamblers, he might not care about getting any other information. There are situations in which one item, if answered in the "wrong" way, is enough. Ordinarily, this is not true. The usual situation is that there are many considerations and that the plus and minus features must be weighed before a decision may be made. It is, therefore, important to obtain complete information.

1. According to the above passage, it was generally believed that an interviewer would have difficulty in obtaining the information he sought from a person if he

    A. were tricky in his methods
    B. were open and frank in his approach
    C. were clever in his questioning
    D. utilized carefully prepared questions

2. The passage does NOT reveal whether the type of questions used

    A. trapped those being interviewed
    B. elicited facts which an open method of questioning might miss
    C. elicited the most important facts that were sought
    D. covered matters which those interviewed were reluctant to talk about openly

3. An argument in favor of the *tricky* or *clever* interviewing technique is that, unless this approach is used, the person interviewed will NOT

    A. offer to furnish all pertinent information
    B. answer questions concerning routine data

C. clearly understand what is being sought
D. want to continue the interview

4. According to the above passage, in favorable circumstances, a talented interviewer would be able to obtain from the person interviewed information

   A. which the person regards as irrelevant
   B. which the person intends to conceal
   C. about the person's family background
   D. which the person would normally have forgotten

5. According to the above passage, a highly skilled interviewer should concentrate, in most cases, on getting

   A. one outstanding fact about the interviewee which would do away with the need for prolonged questioning
   B. facts which the interviewee wanted to conceal because these would be the most relevant in making a decision
   C. all the facts so that he can consider their relative values before reaching any conclusion
   D. information about any bad habits of the interviewee, such as gambling, which would make further questioning

Questions 6-8.

DIRECTIONS: Questions 6 through 8 are to be answered SOLELY on the basis of the following passage.

City governments have long had building codes which set minimum standards for building and for human occupancy. The code (or series of codes) makes provisions for standards of lighting and ventilation sanitation, fire prevention and protection. As a result of demands from manufacturers, builders, real estate people, tenement owners, and building-trades unions, these codes often have established minimum standards well below those that the contemporary society would accept as a rock-bottom minimum. Codes often become outdated, so that meager standards in one era become seriously inadequate a few decades later as society's concept of a minimum standard of living changes. Out-of-date codes, when still in use, have sometimes prevented the introduction of new devices and modern building techniques. Thus, it is extremely important that building codes keep pace with changes in the accepted concept of a minimum standard of living.

6. According to the above passage, all of the following considerations in building planning would probably be covered in a building code EXCEPT

   A. closet space as a percentage of total floor area
   B. size and number of windows required for rooms of differing sizes
   C. placement of fire escapes in each line of apartments
   D. type of garbage disposal units to be installed

7. According to the above passage, if an ideal building code were to be created, how would the established minimum standards in it compare to the ones that are presently set by city governments?
They would

A. be lower than they are at present
B. be higher than they are at present
C. be comparable to the present minimum standards
D. vary according to the economic group that sets them

8. On the basis of the above passage, what is the reason for difficulties in introducing new building techniques?   8._____

   A. Builders prefer techniques which represent the rock-bottom minimum desired by society.
   B. Certain manufacturers have obtained patents on various building methods to the exclusion of new techniques.
   C. The government does not want to invest money in techniques that will soon be outdated,
   D. New techniques are not provided for in building codes which are not up to date.

Questions 9-11.

DIRECTIONS: Questions 9 through 11 are to be answered SOLELY on the basis of the following passage.

The agreement under which a tenant rents property from a landlord is known as a lease. Generally speaking, leases are classified as either short-term or long-term in duration. They are further subdivided according to the method used to determine the amount of periodic rent payments. Of the following types of leases in use, the more commonly used ones are the following;

1. The straight or fixed lease is one in which rent may be paid in equal amounts throughout the duration of the lease. These are usually restricted to short-term leasing, or somewhat longer-term if clauses in the lease provide for periodic escalation of payments as the economy shifts.
2. Percentage leasing, used for short-term commercial leasing, provides the landlord with a stipulated percentage of a tenant's gross sales from goods and services sold on the premises, in addition to a fixed amount of rent.
3. The net lease, generally long-term (ten years or more), requires the tenant to pay all operating costs, including real estate taxes and insurance. In a net-net lease, the tenant further agrees to meet mortgage interest and principal payments.
4. An escalated lease, which is a long-term lease, requires rent to be of a stipulated base amount which periodically is subject to escalation in accordance with cost-of-living index scales, or in direct proportion to taxes, insurance, and operating costs.

9. Based on the information given in the passage, which type of lease is MOST likely to be advantageous to a landlord if there is a high rate of inflation? _____ lease.   9._____

   A. Fixed   B. Percentage
   C. Net   D. Escalated

10. On the basis of the above passage, which types of lease would generally be MOST suitable for a well-established textile company which requires permanent facilities for its large operations?
    _____ lease and_____ lease.   10._____

   A. Percentage; escalated   B. Escalated; net
   C. Straight; net   D. Straight; percentage

11. According to the above passage, the ONLY type of lease which assures the same amount of rent throughout a specified interval is the _____ lease. 11.____

    A. straight   B. percentage   C. net-net   D. escalated

Questions 12-14.

DIRECTIONS: Questions 12 through 14 are to be answered SOLELY on the basis of the following passage.

Physical design plays a very significant role in crime rate. Crime rate has been found to increase almost proportionately with building height. The average number of crimes is much greater in higher buildings than in lower ones (equal or less than six stories). What is most interesting is that in buildings of six stories or less, the project size or total number of units does not make a difference. It seems that although larger projects encourage crime by fostering feelings of anonymity, isolation, irresponsibility, and lack of identity with surroundings, evidence indicates that larger projects encompassed in low buildings seem to offset what we may assume to be factors conducive to high crime rates. High-rise projects not only experience a higher rate of crime within the buildings, but a greater proportion of the crime occurs in the interior public spaces of these buildings as compared with those of the lower buildings. Lower buildings have more limited public space than higher ones. A criminal probably perceives that the interior public areas of buildings are where his victims are most vulnerable and where the possibility of his being seen or apprehended is minimal. Placement of elevators, entrance lobbies, fire stairs, and secondary exits all are factors related to the likelihood of crimes taking place in buildings. The study of all of these elements should bear some weight in the planning of new projects.

12. According to the above passage, which of the following BEST describes the relationship between building size and crime? 12.____

    A. Larger projects lead to a greater crime rate.
    B. Higher buildings tend to increase the crime rate.
    C. The smaller the number of project apartments in low buildings, the higher the crime rate.
    D. Anonymity and isolation serve to lower the crime rate in small buildings.

13. According to the passage, the likelihood of a criminal attempting a mugging in the interior public portions of a high-rise building is GOOD because 13.____

    A. tenants will be constantly flowing in and out of the area
    B. there is easy access to fire stairs and secondary exits
    C. there is a good chance that no one will see him
    D. tenants may not recognize the victims of crime as their neighbors

14. Which of the following is IMPLIED by the passage as an explanation for the fact that the crime rate is lower in large low-rise housing projects than in large high-rise projects? 14.____

    A. Tenants know each other better and take a greater interest in what happens in the project.
    B. There is more public space where tenants are likely to gather together.
    C. The total number of units in a low-rise project is fewer than the total number of units in a high-rise project.

D. Elevators in low-rise buildings travel quickly, thus limiting the amount of time in which a criminal can act.

Questions 15-19.

DIRECTIONS: Questions 15 through 19 are to be answered SOLELY on the basis of the following *total annual income adjustment* rules for household income.

The basic annual income is to be calculated by multiplying the total of the current weekly salaries of all adults (age 21 or over) by 52.
Upward and downward adjustments must be made to the basic annual salary to arrive at the *total adjusted annual income* for the household.

UPWARD ADJUSTMENTS

1. Add one-half of total overtime payments in the previous two years.
2. Add that part of the earnings of any minor in the household that exceeded $2,000 in the previous 12 months.

DOWNWARD ADJUSTMENTS

1. Deduct one-third of all educational tuition payments for household members in the previous 12 months.
2. Deduct the expense of going to and from work in excess of $20 per week per household member. This adjustment is made on the basis of the previous 12 months and should be computed for each household member individually for each week in which excess travel expenses were incurred.
3. Deduct that part of child care expenses which exceeded $1000 in the previous 12 months.

15. In household A, the husband has a weekly salary of $390 and the wife has just had her salary increased from $260 to $280 per week. In the previous 12 months, each had a paid continuous vacation of four weeks; the husband had to travel to a secondary work location every fourth week. His travel costs during those weeks were $28 per week. In the previous 12 months, they had child care costs of $980.
What is the total annual adjusted income for the household?

    A. $34,744   B. $34,736   C. $34,552   D. $34,156

16. In household B, the husband has a weekly salary of $360. In the past year, he received overtime payments of $170. In the year before that he received overtime payments of $814. His wife has just begun a job with a weekly salary of $220. As a result of this, annual child care expenses will be $1420.
What is the total annual adjusted income for the household?

    A. $30,160   B. $30,232   C. $30,652   D. $31,216

17. In household C, the husband has a weekly salary of $370, The wife has a weekly salary of $260. They each had expenses of $22 per week when traveling to and from work in the previous 12 months. The husband had an annual paid vacation of five weeks, and the wife had an annual paid vacation of three weeks in the previous year. There is a daughter in college for whom annual tuition payments of $1140 were made in the previous 12 months.
    What is the total annual adjusted income for the household?

    A. $32,172   B. $32,188   C. $32,760   D. $33,348

18. In household D, the husband has a weekly salary of $310, the wife has a weekly salary of $220, and an adult daughter has a weekly salary of $190. The husband received overtime payments of $1260 in the past year. In the year before that, he received no overtime payments. In the past year, there were weekly child care expenses of $140 per week for 47 weeks.
    What is the total annual adjusted income for the household?

    A. $38,070   B. $32,490   C. $31,490   D. $31,230

19. In household E, the husband has a weekly salary of $410. The wife has a weekly salary of $130. During the past year, there were tuition payments of $170 per month for 10 months per year for children in grade school and annual tuition payments of $1540 for a boy in high school.
    What is the total annual adjusted income for the household?

    A. $26,380   B. $26,400   C. $27,000   D. $28,080

20. In the writing of reports or letters, the ideas presented in a paragraph are usually of unequal importance and require varying degrees of emphasis.
    All of the following are methods of placing extra stress on an idea EXCEPT

    A. repeating it in a number of forms
    B. placing it in the middle of the paragraph
    C. placing it either at the beginning or at the end of the paragraph
    D. underlining it

KEY (CORRECT ANSWERS)

1. B	6. A	11. A	16. C
2. C	7. B	12. B	17. B
3. A	8. D	13. C	18. B
4. B	9. D	14. A	19. C
5. C	10. B	15. A	20. B

TEST 3

DIRECTIONS: Each question or incomplete statement is followed by several suggested answers or completions. Select the one that BEST answers the question or completes the statement. *PRINT THE LETTER OF THE CORRECT ANSWER IN THE SPACE AT THE RIGHT.*

Questions 1-2.

DIRECTIONS: Questions 1 and 2 are to be answered SOLELY on the basis of the following paragraph.

A housing development has 450 apartments. The average monthly rent is $269 per apartment. The average amount of subsidy money added to the average monthly rent (to meet the total operating costs) is $136. Since the time when the amount of the subsidy was determined, operating costs for the development have increased by $7920.00 per month.

1. If the subsidy is increased by 6%, what increase in the average monthly rental will be necessary to meet monthly operating costs?   1._____

    A. $6.80   B. $9.44
    C. $17.60   D. No increase

2. What is the NEW total monthly operating cost per apartment?   2._____

    A. $153.60   B. $286.60   C. $422.60   D. $484.20

3. In a certain housing project, the average income of tenant families is $18,400 per annum and the average rent per apartment is $360 per month.
If the average income increases 12% in a year while the average rent of an apartment increases 15%, how much more money will the average family have in a year after paying rent?   3._____

    A. $677.60   B. $1560.00   C. $2241.60   D. $4968.00

4. A certain housing project has 1860 tenant families. It has two playgrounds, both rectangular in shape. One measures 104 feet by 45 feet; the other is 74 feet by 53 feet.
The number of square feet of playground space per family in this project is MOST NEARLY   4._____

    A. 3   B. 5   C. 7   D. 9

5. A particular housing project has 1460 occupied apartments. If there are 12 new tenants in January, 14 in February, and 16 in March, the turnover rate for the first quarter of the year is MOST NEARLY   5._____

    A. 2.9%   B. 3.2%   C. 3.5%   D. 3.8%

Questions 6-7.

DIRECTIONS: Questions 6 and 7 are to be answered SOLELY on the basis of the following paragraph.

A tenant in a housing development receives a semi-monthly public assistance check of $234 and pays a monthly rental of $142 from the proceeds. The tenant is about to begin paying $18 additional per month toward total rent arrears of $272. At the same time that the arrears payments begin, his semi-monthly check increases to $242.

6. What will be the TOTAL change in monthly net income after all rent payments. 6._____

    A. $6   B. $4   C. $2   D. No change

7. If, instead of paying only $18 per month toward the arrears, the total increase in public assistance payments is used to increase arrears payments, how many months will it take the tenant to pay off the arrears? 7._____
    _____ months.

    A. 8   B. 10   C. 12   D. 14

8. A tenant is offered two options in renewing a lease: (1) a one-year lease at a 10% increase in rent, or (2) a three-year lease at an 18% increase in rent. The tenant's current rent is $440 monthly. 8._____
    If the tenant takes the first option and continues to live in the apartment for three years with a 10% increase in rent each year, what would be the difference between the total rent he would pay and the rent he would have paid had he chosen the three-year lease?

    A. $533.28   B. $553.28   C. $2,851.20   D. $3,384.48

9. A certain task that an assistant performs takes approximately 45 minutes per unit of work. Seventy-five percent of his work day is spent on this task. 9._____
    Assuming that he works seven hours per day, how many work-days will it take him to finish 1,470 units of work?

    A. 153   B. 210   C. 240   D. 270

10. It takes 5 1/2 gallons of paint to paint an average apartment, and it requires 18 man-hours. 10._____
    If the price of paint increases 24 cents per gallon and the pay of the painters increases 26.5 cents per hour, what is the INCREASE in the cost of painting an apartment?

    A. $4.99   B. $5.09   C. $5.99   D. $6.09

11. A government employee can process a certain type of report in 23 minutes. How many such reports could he finish processing in a work day from 9:00 A.M. to 5:00 P.M., with a 45-minute lunch break and two 10-minute coffee breaks? 11._____

    A. 16   B. 17   C. 18   D. 19

12. The income of a tenant family is as follows: The husband has a gross income of $280 per week; the wife has a gross income of $220 per week. Deductions from gross family income total $116 per week, plus an allowable child care expense of $56 per week. What is the net annual income of the family after deductions and allowable child care expenses? 12._____

    A. $16,656   B. $17,056   C. $18,656   D. $19,056

Questions 13-15

DIRECTIONS: Questions 13 through 15 are to be answered on the basis of the following information and schedule.

Assume that, after having been appointed as an assistant at the Rumsey Housing Project, you are now ready to assume the same duties being performed by the other two assistants, X and Y, Their daily work schedules have already been prepared, and you are asked to work out a schedule which will be compatible with theirs and which will conform to the following stipulations:

    a. At least one assistant is to be in the project office at all times between 9 A.M. and 5 P.M. Monday through Friday.
    b. No more than two assistants are to conduct office interviews at one time.
    c. All assistants must be in the project office between the hours of 4 P.M. and 5 P.M.
    d. Each assistant is to take one hour for lunch between 11:30 A.M. and 2 P.M.
    Following is the Monday schedule for assistants X and Y.

	9am–11am	11am–12pm	12pm–1pm	1pm–2pm	2pm–3pm	3pm–4pm	4pm–5pm
X	Review week-end's material; plan work	Office interviews	Office interviews	Lunch	Desk work; record-keeping	Tenant apartment visits	Office interviews
Y	Office interviews	Office interviews	Plan work	Lunch	Tenant apartment visits	Tenant apartment visits	Desk work; record-keeping

13. Which one of the following blocks of time would be BEST for you to plan 2 1/2 hours of office interviewing?

    A. 9:00-11:30   B. 11:00-1:30
    C. 1:30-4:00   D. 2:00-4:30

14. During what hours would it be BEST for you to schedule tenant apartment visits covering a two-hour block of time?

    A. 9:00-11:00   B. 10:30-12:30
    C. 1:00-3:00   D. 3:00-5:00

15. Of the following suggestions for scheduling your day's assignments, which one would NOT be acceptable?

    A. Desk work including weekly plans from 9:00-11:00 and 2:00-3:00
    B. Interviews from 11:00-1:00
    C. Lunch from 1:00-2:00
    D. Tenant apartment visits from 3:00-5:00

Questions 16-20.

DIRECTIONS: Questions 16 through 20 are to be answered SOLELY on the basis of the information contained in the following table of apartment availabilities and explanation of *Priority Codes for Admission* column.

PRIORITY CODES AND MAXIMUM ANNUAL INCOME
FOR ADMISSION TO PROJECTS

Division	Projects	Priority Codes for Admission	Maximum Annual Income for Admission			
			One Bedroom	Two Bedrooms	Three Bedrooms	Four Bedrooms
Northern	Allan	1-3Cs 4B	$18,200	$20,000	$21,400	$23,000
	Boston	1-2C; 3-4A	13,600	15,800	18,000	19,800
	Danton	1-2C; 3Bs 4 A	14,800	16,400	18,200	20,200
	Miller	1-3B; 4 A	13,600	15,800	18,000	19,800
	Preston	1-2C, 3B; 4A	16,600	18,800	20,400	22,000
Central	Andrews	1-2D; SB; 4 A	13,600	15,800	18,000	19,800
	Clayton	1-2D, SB, 4 A	13,600	15,800	18,000	19,800
	Ivy Hill	1-3C; 4B	14,800	16,400	18,200	20,200
	Montrose	1-2B, 3-4A	18,200	20,000	21,400	23,000
Eastern	Bryan	1B; 2-4 A	16,600	18,800	20,400	22,000
	Farrar	1C; 2-4A	18,200	20,000	21,400	28,000
	Golden	1-2B; 3-4A	13,600	15,800	18,000	19,800
	Wagner	1B; 2-4A	18,200	20,000	21,400	23,000
Western	Colfax	1-3C; 4B	18,200	20,000	21,400	23,000
	Drexel	1-3B, 4 A	14,800	16,400	18,200	20,200
	Foxton	1-3C; 4A	13,600	15,800	18,000	19,800

EXPLANATION OF PRIORITY CODES FOR ADMISSION COLUMN

The letters A, B, C, and D represent four levels of priority for admission to a project. Level A priority is the most restrictive of the four priority levels and represents the highest level of need; level D priority is the least restrictive of the four priority levels and represents the lowest level of need. An applicant can be admitted only to an apartment with the same level of priority or to an apartment with a lower level of priority. For example, an applicant with a C priority can be admitted to an apartment with a C or D priority but not to an apartment with an A or B priority.

The numbers 1, 2, 3, and 4 represent the number of bedrooms in the apartments. For example, the notation after the Allan project, 1-3C; 4B, means that apartments with from one to three bedrooms have priority level C and apartments with four bedrooms have priority level In the Allan project, only applicants with a priority level of C or higher (levels A and B) can be admitted to apartments with one, two, or three bedrooms and only applicants with a priority level of B or higher (level A) can be admitted to a four-bedroom apartment.

16. An applicant with an annual income of $16,400 needs an apartment with two bedrooms. The applicant has a level B priority. Those projects in the Eastern and Central Divisions which have two-bedroom apartments for which the applicant is eligible are

    A. Allan and Ivy Hill
    B. Montrose, Bryan, and Golden
    C. Ivy Hill and Montrose
    D. Ivy Hill, Montrose, and Farrar

17. What is the LOWEST level of priority an applicant may have in order to be eligible for a three-bedroom apartment in the Western Division if he has an income of $18,200 a year?
    Level

    A. A   B. B   C. C   D. D

18. Which division is MOST restrictive as to the level of priority required for three-bedroom apartments?

    A. Northern   B. Central   C. Eastern   D. Western

19. Which division contains the GREATEST number of projects with two-bedroom apartments in the LEAST restrictive level of priority?

    A. Northern   B. Central   C. Eastern   D. Western

20. How many projects have four-bedroom apartments available to an applicant with an A priority and an income of $22,000?

    A. 3   B. 5   C. 7   D. 12

KEY (CORRECT ANSWERS)

1. B	6. C	11. C	16. C
2. C	7. A	12. B	17. C
3. B	8. A	13. D	18. C
4. B	9. B	14. A	19. B
5. A	10. D	15. D	20. C

TEST 4

DIRECTIONS: Each question or incomplete statement is followed by several suggested answers or completions. Select the one that BEST answers the question or completes the statement. *PRINT THE LETTER OF THE CORRECT ANSWER IN THE SPACE AT THE RIGHT.*

Questions 1-4.

DIRECTIONS: Questions 1 through 4 are to be answered SOLELY on the basis of the following information and hypothetical schedule for the granting of priority points. These points determine the applicant's place on a waiting list for an apartment. The applicants may be awarded points for condition of present housing, for children, for veteran status, and for space falling below the minimum space standard. Categories not listed get no points. Points in all categories are added together to determine total number of priority points.

	Priority Points
Condition of Present Housing (choose one)	
Extremely substandard housing	5
Moderately substandard housing	3
Minimally substandard housing	1
Children (choose as many as apply)	
Two children over age eight, of different sexes, sleeping in same room	2
Two children of different sexes, one over age eight, the other under age eight, sleeping in same room	1
Family with child over age 18 months sleeping in same bedroom with parents	2
Veteran Status	
Veteran of Vietnam War in household	1
Minimum Space Standard	
For each 75 square feet or part thereof below minimum space standard, computed by totaling the following:	
110 square feet for each person over age 18	
90 square feet for each person age 18 or under	1

1. A husband, wife, six-year-old son, and nine-year-old daughter live in a moderately substandard apartment of 280 square feet. The son and daughter sleep in the same bedroom. There are no war veterans in the household. How many priority points should be given?

   A. 6   B. 5   C. 4   D. 3

   1._____

2. A husband, wife, wife's father, 16-year-old daughter, 14-year-old son, and 12-year-old son live in an extremely substandard apartment of 450 square feet. The daughter sleeps in her own room. The sons have their own room. The wife's father is a World War II veteran.
   How many priority points should be given?

   A. 9   B. 8   C. 7   D. 6

   2._____

3. A widow, age 50, who is not a war veteran, lives with her son, age 15, in a minimally substandard two-bedroom apartment with 290 square feet of living space.
   How many priority points should be given?

   A. 3   B. 2   C. 1   D. 0

4. A family has had to leave their former apartment because of fire damage. They are presently living in an extremely substandard storefront which is one room of 320 square feet, without partitions. The family consists of a father who is a Vietnam war veteran, a mother, and their two children: a girl, age 5; and a boy, age 7.
   How many priority points should be given?

   A. 10   B. 9   C. 8   D. 7

Questions 5-8.

DIRECTIONS: In Questions 5 through 8, choose the sentence which contains NO errors in grammar, punctuation, or spelling.

5. A. Certain changes in family income must be reported as they occur.
   B. When certain changes in family income occur, it must be reported.
   C. Certain family income changes must be reported as they occur.
   D. Certain changes in family income must be reported as they have been occuring.

6. A. Each tenant has to complete the application themselves.
   B. Each of the tenants have to complete the application by himself.
   C. Each of the tenants has to complete the application himself.
   D. Each of the tenants has to complete the application by themselves.

7. A. Yours is the only building that the construction will effect.
   B. Your's is the only building affected by the construction.
   C. The construction will only effect your building.
   D. Yours is the only building that will be affected by the construction.

8. A. A copy of the lease, in addition to the Rules and Regulations, are to be given to each tenant.
   B. The Rules and Regulations and a copy of the lease is being given to each tenant.
   C. A copy of the lease, in addition to the Rules and Regulations, is to be given to each tenant.
   D. A copy of the lease, in addition to the Rules and Regulations, are being given to each tenant.

Questions 9-10.

DIRECTIONS: Each of Questions 9 and 10 consists of four numbered sentences which constitute a paragraph in a report. They are not in the right order. Choose the numbered arrangement appearing after letter A, B, C, or D which is MOST logical and which BEST expresses the thought of the paragraph.

9. I. Congress made the commitment explicit in the Housing Act of 1949, establishing as a national goal the realization of *a decent home and suitable environment for every American family.*
    II. The result has been that the goal of decent home and suitable environment is still as far distant as ever for the disadvantaged urban family.
    III. In spite of this action by Congress, federal housing programs have continued to be fragmented and grossly underfunded.
    IV. The passage of the National Housing Act signalled a new federal commitment to provide housing for the nation's citizens,

    A. I, IV, III, II
    B. IV, I, III, II
    C. IV, I, II, III
    D. II, IV, I, III

10. I. The greater expense does not necessarily involve *exploitation,* but it is often perceived as exploitative and unfair by those who are aware of the price differences involved, but unaware of operating costs.
    II. Ghetto residents believe they are *exploited* by local merchants and evidence substantiates some of these beliefs.
    III. However, stores in low-income areas were more likely to be small independents, which could not achieve the economies available to supermarket chains and were, therefore, more likely to charge higher prices, and the customers were more likely to buy smaller-sized packages which are more expensive per unit of measure.
    IV. A study conducted in one city showed that distinctly higher prices were charged for goods sold in ghetto stores than in other areas.

    A. IV, II, I, III
    B. IV, I, III, II
    C. II, IV, III, I
    D. II, III, IV, I

11. If an assistant is writing to an applicant who is a minority group member in reference to his eligibility for an apartment, it would be BEST for him to use language that is

    A. informal, using ethnic expressions known to the applicant
    B. technical, using the expressions commonly used in the housing authority
    C. simple, using words and phrases which laymen understand
    D. formal, to remind the applicant that he is dealing with a government agency

12. Assume that you have just informed an applicant for an apartment that he has a low priority and that it is unlikely that he will be assigned an apartment within the next two years. When informed of this, he becomes angry and abusive.
    Of the following, the MOST effective action you can take is to

    A. tell the applicant that you will do your best to get him a higher priority
    B. let him know he cannot intimidate you
    C. tell him to submit a new application that has greater emotional appeal
    D. keep your self-control and try to calm the applicant

13. When interviewing an applicant to determine his eligibility for public housing, it is MOST important to

    A. have a prior mental picture of the typical eligible applicant
    B. conduct the interview strictly according to a previously prepared script
    C. keep in mind the goal of the interview, which is to determine eligibility
    D. get an accurate and detailed account of the applicant's life history

14. The practice of trying to imagine yourself in the applicant's place during an interview is

    A. *good,* mainly because you will be able to evaluate his responses better
    B. *good,* mainly because it will enable you to treat him as a friend rather than an applicant
    C. *poor,* mainly because it is important for the applicant to see you as an impartial person
    D. *poor,* mainly because it is too time-consuming to do this with each applicant

15. When dealing with tenants from different ethnic backgrounds, an assistant should be aware of certain tendencies toward prejudice.
    Which of the following statements is LEAST likely to be valid?

    A. Whites prejudiced against Blacks are more likely to be prejudiced against Puerto Ricans than whites not prejudiced against Blacks.
    B. The less a white is in competition with Blacks, the less likely he is to be prejudiced against them.
    C. Persons who have moved from one social group to another are likely to retain the attitudes and prejudices of their original social group.
    D. When there are few Blacks or Puerto Ricans in a project, whites are less likely to be prejudiced against them than when there are many.

16. Mr. Smith asks the assistant why his rent is higher than his neighbor's, although he claims that both apartments are the same size, and that his neighbor's income is the same as his. The assistant is aware of this but is also aware that the neighbor is allowed several deductions in computing income that are not available to Mr. Smith.
    The assistant should explain to Mr. Smith that

    A. the amount of his neighbor's rent is really no concern of his, but that the neighbor's rent will be raised if Mr. Smith can prove that the neighbor is not reporting income
    B. his neighbor receives more deductions in computing income
    C. he cannot discuss complaints presented by Mr. Smith concerning the rent of other tenants
    D. the amount of rent is based on the rules for computing rent and that there may be individual circumstances of which Mr. Smith is not aware

17. Of the following, the assistant who is MOST likely to be a good interviewer of people seeking low-rent housing from a public agency is one who

    A. tries to get applicants to seek private housing instead
    B. believes that it is necessary to get as much pertinent information as possible in order to determine the applicant's real needs
    C. believes that people who seek public housing are likely to have persons with a history of irresponsible behavior in their households
    D. is convinced that there is no need for public housing

18. An assistant must be familiar with the policies of both federal and state agencies which regulate public housing as well as with the many rules, regulations, and procedures of the housing authority.
The MOST important reason for an assistant to have a thorough knowledge and understanding of these policies and procedures is that he 18.____

    A. will know when to tell an applicant that his request for a particular project cannot be granted
    B. will be able to back up his actions by referring to the relevant rule or policy when making a report
    C. can give the best possible service to tenants and applicants
    D. will be able to show that he has the knowledge needed for his job

Questions 19-20.

DIRECTIONS: Questions 19 and 20 must be answered SOLELY on the basis of the following passage.

The new suburbia that is currently being built does not look much different from the old; there has, however, been an increase in the class and race polarization that has been developing between the suburbs and the cities for several generations now. The suburbs have become the home for an ever larger proportion of working-class, middle-class, and upper-class whitest the oities, for an even larger proportion of poor and non-white people. A great number of cities are 30 to 50 percent non-white in population, with more and larger ghettos than cities have ever had. Now, there is greater urban poverty on the one hand, and stronger suburban opposition to open housing and related policies to solve the cities' problems on the other hand. The urban crisis will worsen, and although there is no shortage of rational solutions, nothing much will be done about the crisis unless white America permits a radical change of public policy and undergoes a miraculous change of attitude towards it cities and their populations.

19. Which of the following statements is IMPLIED by the above passage? 19.____

    A. The percentage of non-whites in the suburbs is increasing.
    B. The policies of suburbanites have contributed to the seriousness of the urban crisis.
    C. The problems of the cities defy rational solutions.
    D. There has been a radical change in the appearance of both suburbia and the cities in the past few years.

20. Of the following, the title which BEST describes the passage's main them is: 20.____

    A. The New Suburbia
    B. Urban Poverty
    C. Urban-Suburban Polarization
    D. Why Americans Want to Live in the Suburbs

KEY (CORRECT ANSWERS)

1. A	6. C	11. C	16. D
2. C	7. D	12. D	17. B
3. C	8. C	13. C	18. C
4. A	9. B	14. A	19. B
5. A	10. C	15. C	20. C

EXAMINATION SECTION
TEST 1

DIRECTIONS: Each question or incomplete statement is followed by several suggested answers or completions. Select the one that BEST answers the question or completes the statement. *PRINT THE LETTER OF THE CORRECT ANSWER IN THE SPACE AT THE RIGHT.*

Questions 1-15.

DIRECTIONS: In answering Questions 1 through 15, assume, unless otherwise indicated, that you are a housing assistant in a public housing project. For each item, select the answer which you believe to be the acceptable one among those listed.

1. During an interview in which a tenant's annual income is being verified, the tenant asks your advice on handling a matter of considerable financial importance to her.
   Of the following, the MOST advisable action for you to take is to

   A. refer the tenant to your superior who has had much wider experience in such matters
   B. explain to the tenant that you cannot advise her on personal matters
   C. ask the tenant if she wishes you to refer her to a legal aid organization
   D. discuss the matter with her in order to clarify the problem so that she will be able to make her own decision

2. In spite of the fact that all tenants have been reminded by letter that no garbage may be left in the hallway in front of the incinerator, this still happens occasionally. Of the following, the MOST advisable action to take next in order to eliminate this practice is to

   A. send another letter to all the tenants but word it very strongly
   B. call a meeting of all the tenants to emphasize the necessity of following this rule
   C. post signs of warning in the incinerator hallway
   D. have the maintenance staff keep a continuous close watch in order to determine who the offenders are so that they may be dealt with properly

3. During an interview, a tenant asks you why another tenant living in an apartment with the same number of rooms pays less rent than she does.
   The MOST advisable action for you to take is to

   A. advise the tenant that you will investigate her statement and, if true, an adjustment will be made
   B. explain to the tenant the reason for the difference in rent
   C. inform the tenant that you cannot discuss with her the rent paid by other tenants
   D. tell the tenant that complaints of this sort should be made to the central office of the Housing Authority

4. One of your tenants asks you to lend her $10 so that she will have enough money to be able to pay her rent. Her rent payments have always been on time in the past, and the sincerity of her explanation of the situation is apparent to you.
   Of the following, the MOST advisable action for you to take is to

1.____

2.____

3.____

4.____

A. express your sympathy for her plight but explain that you do not have that much money to spare until she can repay it
B. lend her the money if you can spare it but report the matter to your superior
C. refer the tenant to a public or private social welfare agency
D. refuse her request and explain why

5. In the course of an interview with an applicant, who is found to be ineligible for public housing, you tell him that the rental of a certain type of apartment is $200, whereas the correct figure is $190. You discover this mistake after the applicant has left and immediately notify your superior.
The MOST desirable action to be taken in regard to this matter is to

A. ask the applicant to come in for another interview
B. do nothing since the applicant is not eligible
C. hold a staff conference to emphasize that more care must be taken in the future
D. send a letter of explanation to the applicant

6. While walking on the project grounds, you overhear two tenants making derogatory remarks about another tenant. It would be advisable for you to

A. ascertain, if possible, whether these remarks are true before doing anything
B. pay no attention to the incident
C. pay no attention to the incident unless the tenants involved are handled by you
D. tactfully interrupt the conversation and explain that such gossip is detrimental to the spirit of the project

7. A regulation has recently been established which has aroused considerable antagonism among many of the tenants. You are required to enforce this regulation in the course of your duties.
The MOST advisable action for you to take first in this matter is to

A. explain to the tenants the reason for the regulation and the need to follow it
B. refer the matter to your supervisor
C. point out to the tenants that their leases require them to adhere to such regulations as may be established
D. seek the cooperation of the tenants in following established regulations

8. Several of the tenants have complained to you that the increased cost of living has made it difficult for them to pay their rent, and they believe their rents should be lowered.
The MOST advisable course of action for you to take first is to

A. find out the amount of increase in the cost-of-living index since the rent schedules were established in order to have a factual basis for any action necessary
B. tell the tenants you will report their complaints to your supervisor
C. tell the tenants to write to the State Housing Division since that agency has jurisdiction over rent schedules
D. tell the tenants to write to the central office of the City Housing Authority

9. In his relationships with the tenants of a project, the housing assistant should

A. adjust his speech pattern to the cultural level of the tenant with whom he is dealing
B. base all his actions on a strict observance of established rules and policies

C. draw upon the prestige of his position in solving problems which arise
D. give greater consideration to tenants with lower incomes as a compensatory measure

10. In dealing with tenants of housing projects, a general policy of treating all tenants alike is

    A. *undesirable* because it fails to take into account the underlying psychological theory of individual differences
    B. *undesirable* because it substitutes impersonal routine for the fine personal relationships which should be fostered
    C. *desirable* because rules and regulations then become more meaningful
    D. *desirable* because granting special permission to any one tenant will lead to similar requests by other tenants

11. When minor infractions of the rules occur, it is GENERALLY desirable for management to

    A. be just as much concerned with their correction as when the infractions are more serious in nature
    B. be lenient since no great damage is involved
    C. overlook them
    D. undertake a comprehensive educational program to remedy the situation

12. During an interview with a tenant, you find it necessary to refer to certain information contained in the tenant's folder, and you ask the file clerk to get it for you from the files. He tells you that he is too busy to get the material for you.
    Of the following, the BEST course of action for you to take first is to

    A. get the folder yourself, if you can
    B. order the file clerk to interrupt his present work and get the material for you
    C. report the matter to his supervisor
    D. reprimand the file clerk in order to preserve your prestige with the tenant

13. If a housing assistant notices that one part of one of the project buildings is nearly always dirty, he should

    A. pay no attention to the matter since cleanliness of the building is the job of the maintenance staff
    B. report the matter to his supervisor
    C. reprimand the maintenance man assigned to the particular area
    D. supervise the particular area very closely to determine how it happens

14. You have been given a job assignment with a full explanation of how it is to be done. However, when you start doing the job, you realize that the explanation is not completely clear to you.
    Of the following, the MOST advisable course of action for you to take is to

    A. ask the more experienced housing assistants in the office for their interpretation
    B. inform your supervisor of the situation and ask for clarification
    C. perform the job to the best of your ability, in accordance with the instructions given
    D. take no immediate action but bring the matter up *tact*fully at the next staff conference

15. If a housing assistant feels that a certain procedure which is being used is inefficient and can be improved, it would be advisable for him to

    A. discuss the procedure with the other housing assistants who do the same work
    B. wait until the staff is asked for suggestions before bringing up the matter
    C. do nothing about it since the responsibility for such action lies with his superior
    D. do nothing about it since there may be other reasons, with which he is unfamiliar, for using the procedure

15.____

Questions 16-30.

DIRECTIONS: Each of Questions 16 through 30 consists of an italicized word followed by four suggested definitions. Indicate the definition that is MOST NEARLY the same as that of the italicized word in each group.

16. *garrulous*
    A. excited   B. questioning   C. silly   D. talkative

16.____

17. *admonish*
    A. remember   B. silence   C. urge   D. warn

17.____

18. *ostensible*
    A. avowed   B. chief   C. extended   D. real

18.____

19. *precarious*
    A. careless   B. thin   C. uncertain   D. undesirable

19.____

20. *indigent*
    A. destitute   B. disreputable   C. lazy   D. stingy

20.____

21. *acrimonious*
    A. bitter   B. loud   C. rich   D. unjustified

21.____

22. *infer*
    A. assume   B. conclude   C. indicate   D. state

22.____

23. *fortuitous*
    A. accidental   B. desirable   C. fortunate   D. strong

23.____

24. *lugubrious*
    A. middle-aged   B. mournful   C. ridiculous   D. sarcastic

24.____

25. *ponderous*
    A. critical   B. effortless   C. heavy   D. solid

25.____

26. *plenary*
    A. authoritative   B. executive
    C. full   D. important

26.____

27. *laconic*

    A. deliberate   B. inattentive   C. short   D. wise

28. *invidious*

    A. deceptive   B. offensive   C. poor   D. serious

29. *desultory*

    A. aimless   B. loathsome   C. stifling   D. uninterested

30. *trenchant*

    A. besieging   B. dissimilar   C. hidden   D. sharp

31. Statistics on housing frequently use the term *persons per room* as a measure of the degree of overcrowding. This term is ordinarily understood to refer to the figure obtained by dividing the total number of

    A. persons in the family by the total number of rooms used as bedrooms
    B. persons in the family by the total number of rooms used in the house exclusive of bathrooms
    C. adults in the family by the total number of rooms in the house exclusive of bathrooms
    D. persons in the family by the total number of all rooms in the house, including bathrooms

32. The term *site coverage,* as it is usually used in reference to housing projects, means the area occupied by the

    A. buildings alone divided by the total area of the project
    B. buildings and recreation areas divided by the total area of the project
    C. buildings and recreation areas divided by the total area of the project excluding streets
    D. present buildings divided by the area occupied by the buildings previously on the site

33. The term *shelter rent,* as used in connection with housing projects, is GENERALLY understood to refer to the

    A. average rent paid in a project
    B. rentals paid by the tenants
    C. rentals paid by the tenants exclusive of utility costs
    D. rentals paid by the tenants plus the amount of the subsidy required

34. The additional rent payment required to be paid by a tenant in a public housing project, over and above the basic rent of his apartment, as a result of his increased income is known as _____ rent.

    A. adjusted   B. gross   C. surcharge   D. unsubsidized

35. A maintenance employee tells you that he has taken care of a tenant's complaint by fixing a defective trap.
The term *trap,* as generally used, refers to a part of the

A. gas range
B. lighting system
C. plumbing system
D. refrigerator

36. The police power of the state to enforce protective measures for its citizens is constantly enlarging. Society must set up the standards under which it wishes to live. Such standards must include provisions for the housing of the workers under conditions which not only assure safety and health, but also permit of self-respect and dignity.
On the basis of this statement, one would be justified in stating that

    A. limits must be placed on the all-inclusive powers of the state in order to protect private enterprise
    B. social legislation is as necessary as good housing
    C. society has the responsibility of providing adequate subsidized housing for the slum dweller
    D. the state is properly responsible for determining the conditions under which new housing may be constructed

37. A survey of a certain city indicated that about 29% of the population live in one type of substandard area which covers 11% of the city area and is responsible for 4 1/2% of the tax deficit. Also, another 9% of the population live in another low-rental area which covers 2% of the city area and is responsible for 21% of the tax deficit.
On the basis of this statement, it would be MOST correct to state that

    A. most of the city's tax deficit occurs in substandard districts
    B. most of the city's population lives in districts where tax receipts are less than municipal costs
    C. industrial and slum districts account for most of the city's problems
    D. high class residential districts occupy only a very small percentage of the city's area

38. Expansion, succession, and mobility have played a part in determining the social characteristics of the slum. The immigrant populations that have poured into transitional zones of American cities have not sought the slum, have not created slums, but have been forced by their low economic status to live in the low-rental dwellings created in these zones by the city's expansion. The variety of cultural backgrounds immigrant groups have brought with them have contributed to the cultural confusion of the slum. On the basis of this statement, the LEAST accurate of the following statements is:

    A. As the population of a city expands and moves out of certain areas, these areas tend to change in character
    B. Slums have been created by the variety of immigrant cultural backgrounds
    C. The low earnings of immigrants have forced them into housing left behind in the expansion process
    D. The cultural confusion of the slum existed before the influx of immigration

39. A general area in which unsanitary or substandard housing conditions exist may include land, either improved or unimproved, and buildings or improvements not in themselves unsanitary or substandard. Demolition or rehabilitation of the latter may be necessary for effective replanning or reconstruction of the entire area.
On the basis of this statement, it would be MOST accurate to state that

A. an area may be considered substandard from the housing viewpoint even though it contains some acceptable housing
B. in replanning an entire area, little if any consideration need be given to buildings or improvements not in themselves unsanitary or substandard
C. it is not easy to determine the exact boundaries of slum areas
D. under existing law, only substandard dwelling quarters may actually be demolished

40. The slum is not only a grimy mass of brick and mortar that can be torn down and demolished, it is also a way of living -- a whole series of habits, attitudes, and sentiments. On the basis of this statement, it would be MOST correct to state that

   A. demolition of substandard housing in slum areas will provide the basis for a new way of living
   B. desirable urban community life is menaced by the existence of a social class forced into inferior housing and living standards
   C. substandard housing and inferior living conditions constitute social problems of the first magnitude
   D. the slum is imprinted in the lives of the people that occupy it, both adults and children

Questions 41-45.

DIRECTIONS: Carefully study the table below. You are to answer Questions 41 through 45 SOLELY on the basis of the data given in the table.

NUMBER OF PRIVATELY AND PUBLICLY FINANCED DWELLINGS BUILT

Year	PRIVATELY FINANCED				Total Publicly Financed	Total
	One-Family	Two-Family	Multi-Family	Total		
2002	267,000	16,000	49,000	332,000	4,000	336,000
2003	316,000	18,000	65,000	399,000	7,000	406,000
2004	373,000	19,000	66,000	458,000	57,000	515,000
2005	448,000	26,000	56,000	530,000	73,000	603,000
2006	533,000	28,000	58,000	619,000	96,000	715,000
2007	252,000	18,000	31,000	301,000	196,000	497,000
2008	136,000	18,000	30,000	184,000	166,000	350,000
2009	115,000	11,000	13,000	139,000	30,000	169,000
2010	184,000	9,000	15,000	208,000	18,000	226,000
2011	590,000	24,000	48,000	662,000	114,000	776,000
2012	745,000	34,000	72,000	851,000	3,000	854,000

41. Multi-family private dwellings have been built in greater numbers than two-family private dwellings. For the years covered by the table, this statement

   A. is true
   B. is false
   C. is partly true
   D. cannot be determined from the table

42. Considering only the last ten years of the table, the number of years in which the number of one-family private dwellings exceeded the number of publicly-financed dwellings is

    A. 1   B. 2   C. 9   D. 10

43. The number of years during which the number of publicly-financed dwellings was more than half the number of privately financed dwellings is

    A. 1   B. 2   C. 3   D. 4

44. The number of years during which privately-financed one-family dwellings was less than half the total number of all dwellings is

    A. 1   B. 2   C. 3   D. 4

45. The number of years during which there was an increase of at least 10% in the number of private two-family dwellings built is

    A. 1   B. 2   C. 3   D. 4

46. Assume that 135,200 new applications were received in a certain year for the 9,500 apartments made available in new projects. In addition, 32,900 old applications were reviewed for eligibility for the new apartments. Of these, 49,300 new and 9,400 old applicants were found eligible. The percentage of eligible applicants who will NOT receive an apartment is

    A. under 75%
    B. between 75% and 80%
    C. between 80% and 85%
    D. over 85%

47. A project tenant who is a cabdriver works on a commission basis, receiving 42 1/2% of the fares. In addition, his earnings from tips are valued at 29% of the commissions.
    If his average monthly fares equal $2,600, then his annual earnings are

    A. between $15,000 and $17,000
    B. between $17,000 and $19,000
    C. between $19,000 and $21,000
    D. over $21,000

48. A project tenant's earning record for the year is as follows: up to January 15, unemployed, continuously employed for the rest of the year; from Monday, January 16, $215 a week; from Monday, April 3, $195 a week; from Monday, October 2, $225 a week.
    This tenant's income is MOST NEARLY

    A. $7,500   B. $8,750   C. $10,000   D. $11,250

49. In a certain city in 2015, the average cost of constructing one apartment of a public housing project was $51,000, an increase of 4% over 2014.
    The cost of constructing a project of 1,500 apartments in 2015 was more than in 2014 by an amount which is MOST NEARLY

    A. $2,400,000
    B. $2,460,000
    C. $2,940,000
    D. $3,060,000

50. A unit of ten housing assistants has been assigned the job of interviewing 1,800 appli- 50.____
cants. They are each able to do two interviews an hour. After the job is one-third done, an
improvement in the procedure is put into effect which makes it possible to save 25% of
the time.
The number of seven-hour days required for the entire job is MOST NEARLY

    A. 10   B. 11   C. 12   D. 13

KEY (CORRECT ANSWERS)

1. B	11. B	21. A	31. B	41. A
2. C	12. A	22. B	32. A	42. C
3. B	13. B	23. A	33. C	43. B
4. D	14. B	24. B	34. C	44. A
5. D	15. A	25. C	35. C	45. D
6. B	16. D	26. C	36. D	46. C
7. A	17. D	27. C	37. A	47. B
8. B	18. A	28. B	38. B	48. C
9. B	19. C	29. A	39. A	49. C
10. D	20. A	30. D	40. D	50. B

TEST 2

DIRECTIONS: Each question or incomplete statement is followed by several suggested answers or completions. Select the one that BEST answers the question or completes the statement. *PRINT THE LETTER OF THE CORRECT ANSWER IN THE SPACE AT THE RIGHT.*

1. The manager of the project has asked you to compute the cost of 175 feet of electric wire needed for an installation in the project community room. This wire is listed in the catalog in 1000-foot coils, each coil weighing 32 pounds and costing $7.60 a pound.
   The cost of the wire to be used is MOST NEARLY

   A. $29.00   B. $39.60   C. $41.60   D. $42.60

2. One section of a project containing 800 apartments was constructed at a cost of $46,400 per apartment. The two remaining sections of the project, containing 625 apartments each, are still to be built.
   In order that the average construction cost per apartment for the entire project will not exceed $52,000, the cost per apartment in the two sections still to be built should be APPROXIMATELY

   A. $52,400   B. $54,000   C. $55,600   D. $56,000

3. A certain project contains 57 two-room apartments (for two persons), 305 three-room apartments (for three persons), 309 four-room apartments (for four persons), 104 five-room apartments (for four persons), 197 five-room apartments (for five persons), and 52 five-room apartments (for six persons).
   The percentage of four-person apartments in this project is between

   A. 10 and 19.9   B. 20 and 29.9
   C. 30 and 39.9   D. 40 and 49.9

4. Assume that each year the value of a certain project depreciates 2 1/2% of its original value.
   At the end of the third year, its value, after depreciation, is $6,734,900. The original value was MOST NEARLY

   A. $7,252,000   B. $7,253,000   C. $7,280,000   D. $7,290,000

5. A housing project with A apartments contains a total of R rooms. The total number of residents is N.
   The number of residents per apartment is expressed by

   A. N/A   B. R/A   C. A/N   D. N/R

6. A study of slums and housing with special reference to the city was written by

   A. Edmond B. Butler
   B. Miles Colean
   C. James Ford
   D. National Association of Housing Officials

7. The one of the following books in which the BEST description of, and criticism and comment on, the low-rent housing program of the Public Works Administration may be found is

   A. HOUSING AND THE HOUSING PROBLEM by Carol Aronovici
   B. INTRODUCTION TO HOUSING by Edith E. Wood
   C. THE FUTURE OF HOUSING by Charles Abrams
   D. THE NEW DAY IN HOUSING by Louis H. Pink

7.____

8. Some of the duties and responsibilities of a housing manager are reported from actual experience in THE DIARY OF A HOUSING MANAGER written by

   A. Miles Colean
   B. Raymond M. Foley
   C. Abraham Goldfield
   D. Nathan Straus

8.____

Questions 9-12.

DIRECTIONS: Column I lists four items, numbered 9 through 12, each of which is to be matched with ONE of the choices given in Column II. For each item of Column I, write the letter of the acceptable choice in Column II.

COLUMN I

9. Administration of rent control
10. Provides mortgage insurance (but does not lend money for mortgages)
11. Administration of mortgages held by the Home Owners' Loan Corp.
12. Administration of the slum clearance provisions of Federal housing legislation

COLUMN II

A. Public Housing Administration
B. Office of the Housing Expediter
C. National Housing Agency
D. Home Loan Bank Board
E. Federal Housing Administration

9.____
10.____
11.____
12.____

13. In face-to-face contact with the public, it is MOST important that a housing assistant

    A. be clean and well-groomed
    B. avoid slang and technical terms
    C. have a ready explanation for any complaint
    D. let the citizen break off the conversation

13.____

14. In dealing with the public, a housing assistant should recognize that, in general, people will cooperate with a request when they

    A. understand the reason for the request
    B. will learn a new skill as a result
    C. will not be held responsible for the result
    D. will get assistance in carrying it out

14.____

15. Suppose you receive a complaint over the telephone from a resident of the section. The complaint should be considered

    A. a matter which must be followed up
    B. a matter which will be followed up if the complaint is repeated

15.____

C. evidence of poor functioning of the section
D. unfounded until proven otherwise

16. The cost of the land used for housing projects built by the City Housing Authority under its program of housing without cash subsidy is

    A. *lower* than the land cost for previous subsidized projects because the recent group was generally built on vacant land
    B. *lower* than the land cost for previous subsidized projects because the recent group was built under Federal price controls
    C. *higher* than the land cost for previous subsidized projects because real estate prices have increased since then
    D. *higher* than the land cost for previous subsidized projects because the recent group generally involved slum properties

17. The occupancy tax levied by the city is authorized for the special purpose of providing funds

    A. for the building of housing projects
    B. to guarantee loans made for the building of housing projects
    C. to pay subsidies needed to operate projects at low rents
    D. to relocate families from buildings to be demolished so that housing projects can be built

18. The provisions of the Multiple Dwelling Law apply to housing projects in the city because this law is CHIEFLY applicable to buildings

    A. constructed after 1935
    B. containing living quarters for more than two families
    C. of reinforced concrete construction
    D. six or more stories in height

19. The establishment and revision of zoning regulations in the city as they affect areas in which public housing projects are built is a function of the

    A. City Planning Commission
    B. Department of Housing and Buildings
    C. City Housing Authority
    D. State Division of Public Works

20. Unemployment insurance is under the jurisdiction of the

    A. City   B. State
    C. Federal Government   D. Department of Welfare

21. There is urgent need to proceed as rapidly as possible with the revision of existing zoning regulations, especially as to so-called *unrestricted* districts. These districts, in which much current private building activity is going on, are to all interests and purposes unzoned.
    If the revision referred to in this statement were to be placed in effect, an immediate result would PROBABLY be that

A. blighted areas would be saved and prevented from becoming slums
B. new industrial and business construction would have to conform to whatever regulations are set up
C. slums would be eliminated
D. the unsightly and uneconomic mixture of land uses found in many neighborhoods would disappear

22. The housing problem itself clearly is a consequence of the lack of proper distribution of income and wealth, unemployment, and other economic factors.
On the basis of this statement, it would be MOST correct to state that

A. eradication of unemployment is the key to the housing problem
B. good housing could generally be available for all if every family had adequate income
C. proper distribution of housing is a basic factor in solving the housing problem
D. slums are a direct result of the unavailability of acceptable housing

23. The building of some scattered new housing in a slum area is GENERALLY

A. *undesirable* because the need to adhere to new zoning ordinances will make such construction economically unsound
B. *undesirable* because it will be unable to maintain itself against the surrounding slum
C. *desirable* because it may serve as the focus for an overall improvement of living conditions
D. *desirable* because it may provide an incentive for other new construction

24. The high tax expenditures in slum areas tend to decrease upon the demolition of the slum buildings and the re-housing of the population.
The expenditures which decrease LEAST rapidly are those for

A. delinquency prevention B. fire alarms
C. garbage collection D. street cleaning

25. In order to provide a good recreational program for children of the project, it would GENERALLY be advisable to

A. avoid the practice of having any of the children assist in activity leadership
B. have various activities available at any given time
C. avoid the use of parent assistance
D. have all the children engage in the same activities simultaneously

26. The MOST accurate of the following statements concerning an organized play program for children is:

A. No particular consideration need be given to the neighborhood in which the play area is located
B. The activities should have prizes or awards as major motivation
C. The activities should be of such a nature that they involve participation rather than onlooking
D. The program should be fully planned for the children by the person in charge of the play area

27. A principle of operation of community activities in a housing project is:
    A. Community activities should have the cooperation of the management but should not be controlled by management
    B. Community space and activities should be under the supervision and control of the management
    C. No specific space need be set aside for community activities since better results can be achieved by conducting activities in such space as it is not needed by the management
    D. The management should select the leaders of community activities

28. Adequate open space for recreation is generally provided within or near most housing projects.
    Such space is now provided in projects which receive state aid because it
    A. is required by law
    B. is a major characteristic which distinguishes acceptable housing from slums
    C. is the current policy of the State Division of Housing
    D. will enable recreation to become part of an integrated program of recreational, social, and educational activities

29. The broad recreational needs of adults living in public housing projects need be no concern of the project management.
    This statement is
    A. *true* because adequate commercial recreation facilities are available
    B. *false* because one of management's important responsibilities is to assist in providing for various aspects of community life
    C. *true* because recreation is an individual matter in which management interference is unwarranted
    D. *false* because housing does not refer to physical shelter alone, but also to providing a self-sufficient community

30. Planned suburban growth and development is an essential part of postwar home-building activity.
    This statement is PROBABLY
    A. *true* because such construction makes immediate use of available zoned land
    B. *false* because it calls to take into account the great number of public projects being constructed
    C. *true* because land costs in central city areas are generally too high to permit well-planned groups of small homes
    D. *false* because the rebuilding of neglected, disintegrating neighborhoods is far more necessary socially

31. It has been said that home ownership is a magnificent ideal and that the greatest good would be attained when every family in the country owned its own home.
    The CHIEF limitation of this belief is that
    A. changing economic and labor conditions may cause the loss of much of the home owner's investment
    B. it applies only to ownership of one-family dwellings

C. it would discourage large-scale speculative building activity
D. public housing would then no longer offer serious competition with private construction

32. The one of the following which would be LEAST acceptable as proof of residence at a specific address is

    A. automobile driver's license
    B. gas and electric bill
    C. hospital clinic appointment card
    D. life insurance premium receipt

33. An applicant for low-rent housing advises you that his family has in the past received assistance from several private welfare agencies.
    Of the following, the MOST convenient source of additional information about the family is the

    A. Community Service Society
    B. State Department of Social Welfare.
    C. Social Service Exchange
    D. Welfare Council of the City

34. The head of a family applying for an apartment in a low-rent housing project is a widow who was born in a foreign country, married a citizen of the United States in 1931, and has lived here since then. At the time of her marriage, she was not a citizen of the United States.
    The one of the following which would be required as proof of her citizenship is proof of

    A. naturalization in her own right
    B. her marriage, inasmuch as her husband was a citizen
    C. her marriage and proof of her husband's citizenship
    D. her marriage, together with proof of continuous residence in this country

35. The one of the following laws of learning which would be MOST helpful in securing tenant's compliance with the rules and regulations of a housing project is:

    A. Adults do not learn as rapidly as children
    B. Effective remembrance is based on periodic repetition
    C. Emotional acceptance generally precedes understanding and compliance
    D. Understanding is the basis of compliance

36. The development of a fixed pattern for all initial interviews of applicants for public housing is

    A. *desirable* chiefly because it helps to provide a complete record in the least time
    B. *desirable* chiefly because it permits the development of a uniform procedure and simplifies the training of interviewers
    C. *undesirable* chiefly because it fails to provide for the varying circumstances of individual applicants
    D. *undesirable* chiefly because it sacrifices rapport in order to secure uniformity

37. Of the following methods of beginning an interview with an applicant for an apartment, the MOST desirable is to

    A. allow the applicant to discuss his housing problem
    B. assure the applicant of your interest in his need for housing
    C. discuss the purpose of the interview
    D. discuss some impersonal topic familiar to everyone

38. In order to obtain accurate information when he interviews an applicant for public housing, a housing assistant should NOT

    A. allow the applicant to qualify his answers
    B. anticipate the applicant's answers
    C. ask one question at a time
    D. ask questions at first which are easy for the applicant to answer

39. The time when it is generally considered desirable to add to the record subjective comments concerning an applicant and his family is

    A. during the interview
    B. right after the interview has been concluded and the applicant has left
    C. right after the interview has been concluded but before the applicant has left
    D. at the end of the day, after all interviews have concluded

40. The interviewer's choice of words may determine the success or failure of the interview. To be successful in this respect, the interviewer should be careful to

    A. adjust his terminology to the language level of the applicant
    B. employ expressions similar to those of the applicant
    C. speak in terms which are easily understood
    D. use correct technical terms with such explanations as are necessary

41. During a period of economic adjustment when unemployment is on the rise, the invention of a labor-saving device would, in the long run, be economically and culturally

    A. *unsound* because it would stir up unrest among the organized labor groups
    B. *unsound* because it would result in accelerating unemployment
    C. *sound* because the rise of unemployment is a temporary phenomenon while the labor-saving device would add permanent values
    D. *sound* because it would enable the user to produce more with the small working population still employed

42. Wage rates for women in the United States do NOT match those for men in many industries largely because

    A. women tend to constitute a marginal supply of labor
    B. the social attitude has swung back to the position that *women's place is in the home*
    C. the organized labor movement has modified its traditional stand regarding *equal pay for equal work*
    D. women do not attain highly responsible positions in the business world as consistently as men

43. The inability of people to obtain employment during a time of economic depression is an example of the principle that

    A. anyone who really wants a job can get one if he tries hard enough
    B. the more capable people get jobs when jobs are scarce
    C. at certain times employment is not available for many people irrespective of ability, character, or need
    D. full employment is a thing of the past

44. It is often held that cooperative activity is difficult to achieve because *individuals are basically selfish* and their alleged selfishness makes it difficult, if not impossible, to subordinate their individual wills to the collective enterprise.
    The CHIEF factor overlooked in such a conception of the matter is that

    A. there is no necessary discrepancy or conflict between selfishness and cooperation
    B. the people do not seek to further their self-interest by competitive activity
    C. competition and cooperation are essentially alike
    D. most successful people are not selfish

45. Reports show that more men than women are physically handicapped MAINLY because

    A. women are instinctively more cautious than men
    B. men are more likely to have congenital deformities
    C. women tend to seek surgical remedies because of greater concern over personal appearance
    D. men are more likely to be exposed to hazardous conditions

KEY (CORRECT ANSWERS)

1. D	11. D	21. B	31. A	41. C
2. C	12. A	22. B	32. C	42. A
3. D	13. B	23. B	33. C	43. C
4. C	14. A	24. A	34. A	44. A
5. A	15. A	25. B	35. D	45. D
6. C	16. A	26. C	36. A	
7. C	17. C	27. A	37. C	
8. C	18. B	28. A	38. B	
9. B	19. A	29. B	39. B	
10. E	20. B	30. C	40. C	

EXAMINATION SECTION
TEST 1

DIRECTIONS: Each question or incomplete statement is followed by several suggested answers or completions. Select the one that BEST answers the question or completes the statement. *PRINT THE LETTER OF THE CORRECT ANSWER IN THE SPACE AT THE RIGHT.*

1. While in your office, your attention is attracted by the sound of loud crying. Looking out of the window, you see two small boys, each about ten years old, punching a little girl of about the same age. The incident is taking place off the project grounds but you recognize the children and know they live in the project.
   What is the BEST course of action to take?

   A. Do not interfere since it is off project grounds.
   B. Go out and stop the fighting.
   C. Notify the parents involved.
   D. Separate the children, scold the boys, and take the little girl back with you so the fighting will not recur.
   E. Shout, *"Stop that fighting. Boys, you should be ashamed of yourselves."*

1.____

2. One of the tenants tells you she is sure that the income of a certain family exceeds the permissible maximum.

   A. Ask the tenant how she learned of this information so you may verify it.
   B. Ask the tenant to write out the details and send it to the office.
   C. Notify your superior so he may take appropriate action.
   D. Tell the tenant that stirring up trouble for another family is detrimental to the smooth functioning of the project.
   E. Thank the tenant for the information and tell her you will look into it.

2.____

3. A tenant informs you that he is a member of a group which would like to use the project community room to hold card games on a certain evening each week.

   A. Advise the tenant that it will be permitted if he will assume the responsibility in case there is any gambling.
   B. Advise the tenant to make a written request to the manager.
   C. Ask the tenant for all details before making any decision
   D. Tactfully bring the conversation around to more desirable social activities and indicate that a request for a different activity will then be approved.
   E. Tell the tenant that the community room is already taken on that evening in order to avoid antagonizing him by criticizing the proposed activity.

3.____

4. Several tenants complain to you that they are frequently disturbed late at night by loud radio playing from an adjoining apartment. One or more of these tenants have, on several occasions, asked the neighbor to lower the radio but to no avail.

   A. Advise the tenants that they should complain to the department of health.
   B. Advise the tenants that they should complain to the police department.
   C. Ascertain whether the complaint is justified.
   D. Request the tenant to lower the radio and explain the reason for the request.
   E. Tell the tenants to present the matter at the next meeting of the tenants' association.

4.____

5. A tenant asks you whether it is permissible for him to bring several friends who live outside the project, but near it, to a special educational program which has been scheduled for the project meeting room.

   A. Advise the tenant to ask the manager for permission.
   B. Ask the tenant who his friends are before giving him any answer.
   C. Inform the tenant that he may do so.
   D. Refer the tenant to the president of the tenants' association.
   E. Tactfully explain to the tenant why outsiders are not permitted.

6. A tenant who has never made any previous complaints complains to you that the penetrating cooking odors of a certain tenant are frequently very objectionable.

   A. Arrange to move the tenant at fault to another section of the project.
   B. Ascertain whether the complaint is justified.
   C. Discuss the situation with the complaining tenant.
   D. Discuss the situation with the tenant at fault.
   E. Explain to the complaining tenant that you cannot interfere in such personal matters.

7. While walking through the corridor of the project, you see a tenant trip and fall down about half a flight of stairs. The tenant immediately picks himself up, states that he is perfectly all right, and begins to go on about his business.

   A. Advise the tenant to prepare a written statement at his own convenience and send it to the manager.
   B. Ask the tenant to accompany you to the office so he may sign a statement that he suffered no injury.
   C. Insist that the tenant accompany you to a doctor for examination for possible injury.
   D. Submit a report on the occurrence to your supervisor.
   E. Think no more of the situation since obviously no injury was incurred.

8. While walking on the court of the project, you notice a tenant's nine-year-old child destroying some of the shrubbery.

   A. Notify the parent that he will be held financially responsible for damages incurred.
   B. Provide socially desirable outlets for children's activities.
   C. Report the child's behavior to his parents.
   D. Report the incident to your superior so he may take appropriate action.
   E. Reprimand the child.

9. A tenant complains to you that it is very cold in her apartment.

   A. Advise her to make the complaint to the building superintendent.
   B. Ascertain if the complaint is justified.
   C. Pay no attention to the matter unless additional complaints are made by other tenants.
   D. Report the matter to the building superintendent.
   E. Tactfully tell her that it is her problem since heat is being supplied in accordance with the law.

10. A tenant who wants to buy a pressure cooker asks you what brand she should buy.

    A. Inform her that you must be impartial and, therefore, cannot make any recommendation.
    B. Refer her to a consumer cooperative where you know she can get a substantial discount.
    C. Refer her to a department store where a salesman can help her make a selection from the various types which you know they sell.
    D. Refer her to organizations which make comparative tests of consumers' goods.
    E. Tactfully explain that a pressure cooker is a luxury and that a serviceable cooking utensil can be bought for a small fraction of the cost.

11. To say that a housing assistant should apply the pragmatic test to his beliefs means MOST NEARLY that he should be

    A. certain of authoritative sources
    B. familiar with current philosophic thought
    C. guided by practical results
    D. skeptical of generally accepted conclusions
    E. trained in laboratory methods

12. A housing assistant who is *sanguine* is

    A. belligerent   B. cruel   C. lazy
    D. optimistic   E. sound in mind

13. An *abstemious* tenant is a desirable tenant.
    The word *abstemious* means, MOST NEARLY,

    A. adhering punctiliously to established rules and accepted practices
    B. exact in the observance of the usages of polite society
    C. indulging temperately in alcoholic beverages
    D. possessing abundant health and vitality
    E. totally abstaining from intoxicants

14. Public housing is not *indigenous* to the United States. The word *indigenous* means, MOST NEARLY,

    A. competing with housing constructed under private enterprise
    B. looked upon unfavorably
    C. originating in a specific country
    D. restricted to persons receiving public financial assistance
    E. taxable source of revenue

15. The report contained statements which were *equivocal*. The word *equivocal* means, MOST NEARLY,

    A. diametrically opposed
    B. not recognized as valid or authentic
    C. of the same degree in magnitude or value
    D. pertaining to principles of right and justice
    E. susceptible of different interpretations

16. The housing assistant pointed out the *hiatus* in the manual procedures. 16._____
The word *hiatus* means, MOST NEARLY,

    A. error in fact
    B. explanation of policy
    C. incorrect word usage
    D. some part missing
    E. typographical inaccuracy

17. To say that the dose administered to the tenant was *innocuous* means, MOST NEARLY, 17._____
that the dose was

    A. curative
    B. deadly
    C. harmless
    D. painful
    E. protective

18. A tenant who has been subjected to *ostracism* has been, MOST NEARLY, 18._____

    A. a victim of cruel and unusual punishment
    B. excluded from participating in social affairs
    C. exposed to personal indignities
    D. inoculated against contagious diseases
    E. the recipient of the contempt of his neighbors

19. When actions of a tenant are *condoned* by a housing assistant, the actions are, MOST 19._____
NEARLY,

    A. approved
    B. condemned
    C. justified
    D. overlooked
    E. scrutinized

20. To say that a housing assistant sometimes encounters *extenuating* circumstances 20._____
means, MOST NEARLY, that the housing assistant must consider

    A. facts pertinent only to the solution of the problem in hand
    B. facts which lessen the seriousness of an offense
    C. facts which require the immediate attention of his supervisor
    D. situations that call for very tactful handling
    E. situations where legal action is obligatory

21. Suppose you are assigned to make a home investigation of an applicant for an apart- 21._____
ment in a public housing project at a time when there are vacancies. The applicant lives
in grossly substandard housing and appears to be eligible in all respects. He begs you to
tell him if he is eligible.
The one of the following actions you should take is:

    A. Advise him that he keeps his apartment in such poor condition that he will probably
       be refused
    B. Assure him he will get an apartment since he meets the eligibility requirements
    C. Inform him that he will be notified of the status of his application as soon as it is
       acted upon
    D. Tell him that you are not permitted to inform him of the results of your investigation
    E. Tell him you will check with your office and let him know the next day

22. Suppose you are assigned to investigate an applicant for an apartment in a low-rent public housing project. He is 67 years old and works for a small firm whose only other employee is an office worker. You uncover certain facts which lead you to believe that the applicant's income exceeds the permissible maximum.
The one of the following which is PROBABLY least likely to be available as an indication of the applicant's real income is:

    A. state unemployment insurance records
    B. Social Security Board records
    C. sworn statement from employer
    D. sworn affidavit from the applicant
    E. withholding tax statement

23. In a certain city, 18,250 new dwelling units were built in 1986, thereby increasing the total number of dwelling units in the city by 1.6%.
The number of new dwelling units which had to be built in 1987 to maintain the same rate of increase is, MOST NEARLY,

    A. 18,250   B. 18,400   C. 18,500   D. 18,600
    E. an amount which cannot be determined from the given data

24. A housing project is to be erected on a site of S square feet. Unpaid taxes which must be paid on the X buildings now on the site total Y dollars; the cost of demolishing the buildings is estimated at Z dollars.
The cost, per square foot, of the site, when clear of buildings and free of tax delinquency, is

    A. $\dfrac{XY + Z}{S}$ B. $\dfrac{Y + Z}{S}$ C. $S(Z+Y)$ D. $S(XY+Z)$
    E. an expression which cannot be determined from the given data

25. The one of the following acts under the provisions of which financial assistance to housing was FIRST provided by the Federal government is:

    A. United States Housing Act
    B. Emergency Relief and Construction Act
    C. National Industrial Recovery Act
    D. National Housing Act
    E. Home Owners Loan Corporation Act

26. The Mutual Ownership Housing Plan, as originally conceived, is a plan

    A. for the cooperative ownership of a multiple dwelling
    B. sponsored by the Mutual Life Insurance Company to aid home owners
    C. whereby mutual savings banks promote home ownership
    D. whereby tenants of a project may purchase it from the Federal government
    E. whereby the tenants of a building form a housing company to own and operate the building

27. The one of the following statements concerning public low-rent housing projects which is NOT a provision of the United States Housing Act is:

    A. Federal subsidies are conditioned upon local contribution in certain forms equal to at least 20% of the subsidy
    B. Loans must not exceed 90% of the cost of the project
    C. Loans must be repaid within 60 years
    D. Not more than 25% of Federal funds may be expended within any state
    E. slum dwelling units must be eliminated in numbers equivalent to the number of newly constructed dwelling units

28. The permanent consolidation under one agency of all Federal activities relating to housing was accomplished by

    A. the Lanham Act
    B. Presidential executive order in 1942
    C. Reorganization Act of 1946
    D. the United States Housing Act
    E. none of the above

Questions 29-35.

DIRECTIONS: Column I lists seven items, each of which is to be matched with one of the choices given in Column II. For each item of Column I, write in the space at the right the letter in front of the BEST choice in Column II. (The choices in Column II may be used any number of times.)

COLUMN I	COLUMN II
29. Managed war housing projects of the Federal government	A. FHA
30. Insures loans made by private sources for purchase of homes	B. FHLBA
31. Insures loans made by private sources for alteration or repair of homes	C. FPHA
32. Made loans for refinancing delinquent mortgages on private homes	D. HOLC
33. Provides credit reserve for home-mortgaging and home-financing institutions	E. NAHO
34. Administers low-rent public housing subsidies	
35. The only one of the agencies in Column II which is a part of one of the other agencies listed	

36. An applicant for an apartment in a federally-aided low-rent housing project MUST be   36._____

    A. a resident of the state in which the project is located
    B. a citizen of the United States
    C. gainfully employed
    D. living under unsafe or insanitary housing conditions
    E. all of the above

37. It is the present policy of federally-aided public housing projects to grant first preference   37._____
    to eligible applicants who are families

    A. displaced from the site of a slum clearance project
    B. displaced from a site on which the project was built
    C. of men still in military service
    D. of servicemen and of veterans
    E. who lack housing entirely

38. In determining the net family income of a family applying for admission to a low-rent pub-   38._____
    lic housing project, the one of the following which is NOT an allowable deduction is:

    A. Deductions from wages for pension funds if this is required as a condition of employment
    B. Payroll deductions for income tax
    C. Payroll deductions for social security
    D. Payroll deductions for unemployment insurance
    E. Special expenses incident to employment which are not reimbursed by the employer

39. The *20% gap* policy governing admission rents in Federally-aided public housing refers   39._____
    to the fact that in a given community,

    A. rents in public housing must be at least 20% below the rents at which private enterprise is supplying decent and safe dwellings
    B. rents in public housing must not be more than 20% below the rents at which private enterprise is supplying decent and safe dwellings
    C. maximum rent for a given dwelling unit must not be more than 20% greater than the minimum rent
    D. minimum rent for a given dwelling unit must not be more than 20% below the rental for the same accommodations in privately-owned buildings
    E. minimum rent for a given dwelling unit must be at least 20% below the rental for the same accommodations in privately-owned buildings

40. It was NOT a primary purpose of the United States Housing Act to   40._____

    A. alleviate unemployment
    B. make funds available to states for low-rent housing
    C. make credit available to cities for low-rent housing
    D. promote the general welfare of the nation
    E. stimulate construction of dwellings by private enterprise

KEY (CORRECT ANSWERS)

1. B	11. C	21. C	31. A
2. E	12. D	22. A	32. D
3. B	13. C	23. C	33. B
4. D	14. C	24. E	34. C
5. C	15. E	25. B	35. D
6. B	16. D	26. D	36. B
7. D	17. C	27. D	37. D
8. E	18. B	28. E	38. B
9. D	19. D	29. C	39. A
10. D	20. B	30. A	40. E

TEST 2

DIRECTIONS: Each question or incomplete statement is followed by several suggested answers or completions. Select the one that BEST answers the question or completes the statement. *PRINT THE LETTER OF THE CORRECT ANSWER IN THE SPACE AT THE RIGHT.*

Questions 1-6.

DIRECTIONS: Column I lists the titles and authors of six publications, each of which is to be matched with one of the subjects given in Column II. For each item of Column I, write in the space at the right the letter in front of the subject in Column II which BEST expresses the central theme or major area presented in each publication.

COLUMN I

1. AMERICAN HOUSING by 20th Century Fund
2. HOUSING FOR THE MACHINE AGE by Clarence A. Perry
3. HOUSING COMES OF AGE by Straus and Wegg
4. MODERN HOUSING by Catherine Bauer
5. THE FUTURE OF HOUSING by Charles Abrams
6. THEY SEEK A CITY by Bontemps and Conroy

COLUMN II

A. An account of the battle against slums and the progress in public housing
B. Compendium of articles on public housing in the United States
C. Defines adequate shelter and proposes a ten-year budget for better housing in America
D. European housing and American problems from the background of European experience
E. Housing policy of cities, with particular reference to the neighborhood unit idea
F. Official publication of an outstanding organization of persons interested in housing
G. PWA low-rent slum clearance program
H. Study of family and neighborhood life in four slum areas of the city
I. Survey of how the field of housebuilding is organized and operates
J. Study of Black life in a northern city of the United States
K. Very recent study of our housing problems and a program of housing reform
L. Growth of residential segregation and slums and other relevant housing factors in six cities of the United States

1.____
2.____
3.____
4.____
5.____
6.____

Questions 7-16.

DIRECTIONS: Each of Questions 7 through 16 contains five words in capital letters, one of which is NOT in keeping with the meaning which the selection is evidently intended to carry. The five words in capital letters in each selection are reprinted after the selection. Indicate the letter in front of the one of the one of the five words which does MOST to spoil the true meaning of the selection.

7. The MINIMUM amount that can be paid by the FEDERAL government in any year as annual CONTRIBUTIONS to a low-rent housing project under a given contract for financial aid is a FIXED percentage of the total DEVELOPMENT cost of the project.

    A. Minimum   B. Federal   C. Contributions
    D. Fixed   E. Development

7.___

8. The existence and DIMENSIONS of the slums had long been RECOGNIZED by state legislatures and municipalities, but these local public bodies and officers had WASTED their efforts primarily on UNINTEGRATED remedial measures RESTRICTED in character to building and health codes.

    A. Dimensions   B. Recognized   C. Wasted
    D. Unintegrated   E. Restricted

8.___

9. One of the MAJOR purposes of a program of land ASSEMBLY for urban redevelopment is to direct the location of new HOME building to ZONED city land by erasing the margin that seems to favor unused FRINGE land.

    A. Major   B. Assembly   C. Home
    D. Zoned   E. Fringe

9.___

10. Postwar migration of NONFARM families is estimated (by the National Housing Agency) to INCREASE the need for housing construction only to the extent that OUT-MIGRATION from individual localities is so great as to leave an actual DEFICIT of standard housing in those localities AFTER demolition of all sub-standard units.

    A. Nonfarm   B. Increase   C. Out-migration
    D. Deficit   E. After

10.___

11. The choice of a site has GREAT influence on the degree of INTEGRATION the housing project will maintain in the development of long-range COMMUNITY plans. Careful deliberation about the PRESENT and expected future relation of different PROGRAMS to the whole community is necessary if the project is to succeed in being a natural and happy part of its surroundings.

    A. Great   B. Integration   C. Community
    D. Present   E. Programs

11.___

12. FUTURE planning in the field of public housing must have for its goal not only the elimination of slum-blighted areas AND the providing of decent housing to families of low income, but also the opening of new areas for STREET IMPROVEMENT and development CONTINGENT upon the housing program.

    A. Future   B. And   C. Street
    D. Improvement   E. Contingent

12.___

13. In general, farmers of low income are UNABLE to make payments over a period of years which will approximate the CAPITAL cost of an adequate house. Federal contributions would be available to meet INTEREST and other costs with respect to the house. The LOCAL contribution should be adjusted to recognize the LIMITED possibilities for such contributions.

    A. Unable B. Capital C. Interest
    D. Local   E. Limited

14. LOCAL housing authorities have recognized that the COMMUNITY'S worst housing problems often are those connected with MINORITY groups and have already PRODUCED a SMALL proportion of low-rent housing for such families.

    A. Local   B. Community's C. Minority
    D. Produced E. Small

15. The United States Housing Act LIMITS the Federal function to providing financial aid, seeing that the purposes and REQUIREMENTS of the Act are carried out, and COORDINATING COMMUNITIES in the BUILDING and operation of their projects at the lowest cost consistent with the purpose of the housing.

    A. Limits   B. Requirements C. Coordinating
    D. Communities E. Building

16. A SEASONAL plan of maintenance has important ADVANTAGES for the homeowner and represents a LUCRATIVE field for the organization of special service companies which will undertake ALL types of home maintenance work and will maintain a PERMANENT staff of employees for this purpose.

    A. Seasonal B. Advantages C. Lucrative
    D. All   E. Permanent

17. As the population of cities increases, there is a decrease in the proportion of the developed urban land area which is used for

    A. commercial purposes   B. industrial purposes
    C. parks and open areas   D. residential purposes
    E. streets and thoroughfares

18. The statement that building new homes for the upper income groups will thereby create a supply of older buildings for the lower income groups is NOT tenable unless

    A. the concurrent elimination of slum dwellings takes place
    B. the erection of potential new slums is prevented
    C. the housing shortage is replaced by an excess of housing
    D. the low-income groups are unable to afford the buildings thus vacated
    E. private enterprise has the facilities to build for all families in the upper income groups

19. Of the following, the MOST effective way to reduce the monthly cost of home ownership is to secure reductions in

    A. interest rates
    B. maintenance expenses
    C. property taxes
    D. the capital cost of the house
    E. the capital cost of the land

20. If valid criteria have been used in tenant selection for public housing projects, the result MOST likely to be attained is

    A. homogeneity of tenant characteristics will be assured
    B. larger Federal subsidies will be required
    C. neediest families will receive the greatest proportion of aid
    D. the underlying conditions of slums will be ameliorated
    E. management problems will be simplified

21. Impairment of desirability and usefulness resulting from changes in the arts or in design or from external influences which make a property less desirable for continued use is MOST NEARLY a definition of

    A. blight   B. depreciation   C. deterioration
    D. obsolescence   E. slum area

22. A collection of legal requirements, the purpose of which is to protect the safety, health, morals, and general welfare of those in and about buildings is, MOST NEARLY, a definition of the _____ Code.

    A. Administrative   B. Building   C. Legal
    D. Sanitary   E. Welfare

23. The right to expropriate private property for public use is, MOST NEARLY, a definition of

    A. condemnation   B. eminent domain
    C. excess condemnation D. police power
    E. prior lien

24. A study of the social effects of rehousing families from substandard dwellings showed that the GREATEST improvement occurred in the rate of

    A. fatal home accidents
    B. fire costs
    C. infant deaths
    D. juvenile delinquency
    E. new cases of tuberculosis

25. The one of the following which is NOT a major difference between the State and the United States housing laws for permanent low-rent housing projects is the provision concerning the

    A. base upon which maximum amount of subsidy for a given project is computed
    B. creation of housing companies
    C. maximum contributions required from the local political subdivision
    D. maximum duration of subsidy for a given project
    E. maximum percentage of project cost which may be advanced as a loan

26. The Multiple Dwelling Law does NOT contain basic requirements for multiple dwellings with reference to

    A. areas of yards and courts
    B. height and bulk of buildings
    C. sanitation and water closets
    D. strength of fire retarding construction
    E. ventilation and lighting of rooms

Questions 27-32.

DIRECTIONS: Carefully study the table on the following page. It is followed by Questions 27 through 32, which refer to it alone. You are to judge whether on the basis of the data given in the table each item is:
    A. entirely true
    B. entirely false
    C. partly true and partly false
    D. may or may not be true, but cannot be answered on the basis of these data alone

RESIDENTIAL STRUCTURES AND DWELLING UNITS

Area			Residential Structures		Residential Dwelling Units		Occupied Dwelling Units	
			Number	%	Number	%	Number	%
U.S.		TOTAL	29,313,708	100.0	37,325,470	100.0	34,854,532	100.0
I.	Inside metropolitan districts		11,482,330	39.2	18,185,020	48.8	17,217,317	49.4
	A.	Nonfarm	11,413,959	38.9	17,902,692	48.0	16,948,731	48.6
		1. Urban	9,777,222	33.3	16,116,875	43.2	15,308,089	43.9
		2. Rural	1,636,737	5.6	1,785,817	4.8	1,640,642	4.7
	B.	Farm	68,371	.3	282,328	.8	268,586	.8
II.	Outside metropolitan districts		17,831,378	60.8	19,140,450	51.2	17,637,215	50.6
	A.	Nonfarm	10,367,591	35.4	11,780,497	31.5	10,799,242	31.0
		1. Urban	4,490,156	15.3	5,499,477	14.7	5,288,411	15.2
		2. Rural	5,877,435	20.1	6,281,020	16.8	5,510,831	15.8
	B.	Farm	7,463,787	25.4	7,359,953	19.7	6,837,973	19.6

27. In all categories, the figures for urban nonfarm areas represent a greater proportion of the United States total than rural nonfarm areas.

28. The ratio of total residential dwelling units to residential structures is less for nonfarm areas inside metropolitan districts than for such areas outside metropolitan districts.

29. In only one group does the number of unoccupied residential dwelling units exceed 10% of the total number of residential dwelling units.

30. The percentage of occupancy of residential structures with more than one dwelling unit is greater inside metropolitan districts than outside metropolitan districts.

31. In all categories, the figures for urban nonfarm areas, both inside and outside metropolitan districts, represent a greater proportion of the district totals than do rural nonfarm areas.

32. The average number of occupied dwelling units per structure is less in rural nonfarm areas than in the other areas for which data are given.

33. The solution of problems by a display of authority by the housing assistant is

    A. *desirable* because it is a necessary device in making the tenants conform to established policies
    B. *desirable* because it is inherent in his work
    C. *undesirable* because it indicates unwarranted assumption of power
    D. *undesirable* because it is natural only to the aggressive housing assistant
    E. *undesirable* because it violates the principle of delegation of authority

34. When conducting a first interview with an applicant for an apartment who speaks English poorly, the skill of the housing assistant is indicated by

    A. asking the applicant to return the following day when a staff member familiar with the applicant's language will be available
    B. creating a spirit of rapport in spite of the language difficulty
    C. explaining to the applicant how his language handicap affects his eligibility
    D. explaining to the applicant that he would probably find it difficult to get along with the other tenants because of their prejudice against foreigners
    E. impartially discussing the situation with the applicant without any particular consideration of his language background

35. In order to secure information on several specific points from all the tenants of a project, it has been suggested that a questionnaire be distributed to be completed and returned by the tenants.
    The use of such a procedure is GENERALLY

    A. *desirable* because it is a valuable means of building the cooperative relationship which should exist between tenants and management
    B. *desirable* because it provides a written record of each tenant's reply
    C. *undesirable* because distribution and collection of questionnaires is time-consuming
    D. *undesirable* because few tenants will probably fill out the questionnaires incorrectly
    E. *undesirable* because it makes no provision for the expression of related information or viewpoints

KEY (CORRECT ANSWERS)

1. I	11. E	21. D	31. B
2. E	12. C	22. B	32. C
3. G	13. A	23. B	33. C
4. D	14. E	24. A	34. B
5. K	15. C	25. A	35. B
6. L	16. A	26. A	
7. A	17. D	27. B	
8. C	18. C	28. B	
9. D	19. D	29. A	
10. D	20. C	30. D	

EXAMINATION SECTION

TEST 1

DIRECTIONS: Each question or incomplete statement is followed by several suggested answers or completions. Select the one that BEST answers the question or completes the statement. *PRINT THE LETTER OF THE CORRECT ANSWER IN THE SPACE AT THE RIGHT.*

1. A specialist is meeting with a panel of local community leaders to determine their perceptions about the effectiveness of a recent outreach program. The leaders seem unresponsive to the specialist's questions, looking at the floor or each other without directly answering the specialist's questions.
   One strategy that might work to elicit the desired information would be to
   A. try to discern the hidden meaning of their silence
   B. adopt a mildly confrontational tone and remind them of what's at stake in the community
   C. keep asking open-ended questions and wait patiently for responses
   D. tell them to come back when they're ready to tell you their opinions

   1.____

2. Each of the following statements about maintaining a community's attention is true, EXCEPT:
   A. The more challenging it is to pay attention to a message, the more likely it is that it will be attended to
   B. Listeners will be more motivated to pay attention if a speech is personally meaningful
   C. People will be more likely to attend if a speaker pauses to suggest natural transitions in a speech
   D. Listeners will attend to messages that stand out

   2.____

3. Each of the following is a key strategy to integrative bargaining among community members in conflict, EXCEPT
   A. focusing on positions, rather than interests
   B. separating the people from the problem
   C. aiming for an outcome based on an objectively identified standard
   D. using active listening skills, such as rephrasing and questioning

   3.____

4. Which of the following is NOT one of the major variables to take into account when considering a community needs assessment?
   A. State of program development   B. Resources available
   C. Demographics   D. Community attitudes

   4.____

5. Which of the following groups would probably be formed specifically for, or be involved in, the purpose of addressing a specific unmet community need?
   A. An existing consumer group
   B. A council of community representatives
   C. A committee
   D. An existing community organization

   5.____

6. If a public outreach campaign designed to mobilize a community fails, the MOST likely reason for this failure is that the campaign
   A. was not specific about what it wanted people to do
   B. was overly serious and did not appeal to people's sense of humor
   C. offered no incentive for the audience to make a change
   D. did not use language that appealed to the audience's emotions

7. Nationwide, the rate of involvement of elderly people in community-based programs demonstrates that they are
   A. under-served when compared to other age groups
   B. served at about the same rate as other age groups
   C. over-served when compared to other age groups
   D. hardly served at all

8. In projecting the likelihood of an education program's success, a domestic violence specialist identifies every single event that must occur to complete the project. The specialist then arranges these events in sequential order and allocates time requirements for each. Finally, the total time is calculated and a model showing all their events and timelines is charted.
   The specialist has used
   A. a PERT chart
   B. a simulation
   C. a Markov model
   D. the critical path method

9. When working with members of a predominantly African-American community, specialists from other cultural backgrounds should be aware that African-Americans tend to express thoughts and feelings through descriptions of
   A. physically tangible sensations
   B. problems to be analyzed
   C. corresponding analogies
   D. spiritual issues

10. Local nonprofessionals should be considered useful to a specialist who is looking to undertake a community outreach or educational initiative.
    Which of the following is LEAST likely to be a characteristic or role demonstrated by these community members?
    A. Undertaking support functions at the agency
    B. Serving as a communication channel between the agency and clients
    C. Encouraging greater agency acceptance and credibility within the community
    D. Helping the agency to accomplish meaningful change

11. In working with Native American groups or clients, it is important to recognize that the GREATEST health problem facing their communities today is
    A. domestic violence
    B. depression and suicide
    C. alcoholism
    D. tuberculosis

12. A specialist is facilitating a cooperative conflict resolution session between community members who have different opinions about what kinds of intervention services should be offered by the local adult protective services agency.
Which of the following is NOT a guideline that should be followed in this process?
    A. Early in the negotiations, ask each party to name the issues on which they will positively not yield.
    B. Try to get the parties to view the issue from other points of view, beside the two or three conflicting ones.
    C. Have each side volunteer what it would be willing to do to resolve the conflict.
    D. At the end of the session, draw up a formal agreement with agreed-upon actions for both parties.

13. A specialist wants to evaluate the effectiveness of a local women's shelter. The shelter has suffered from lax participation, given the number of women who have been abused in the surrounding area. The specialist wants to speak with the women in the community who did not follow up on referrals to the shelter, and begins by visiting some of these women. After gaining the trust of these women, the specialist asks for the names of women they know who might be in need of help with a domestic violence situation.
The specialist's approach in this case is _____ sampling.
    A. maximum variation   B. snowball
    C. convenience   D. typical case

14. When it comes to perceiving messages, people typically DON'T
    A. tend to simplify causal connections and sometimes even seek a single cause to explain what may be a highly complex effect
    B. tend to perceive messages independently of a categorical framework, especially if the message may be distorted by such an interpretation
    C. have a predisposition toward accepting any pattern that a speaker offers to explain seemingly unconnected facts
    D. tend to interpret things in the way they are viewed by their reference group

15. The elder members of Native American communities, regardless of kinship, are MOST commonly referred to as
    A. the ancients   B. father or mother
    C. grandfather or grandmother   D. chiefs

16. Each of the following is typically an objective of community mobilization, EXCEPT:
    A. To convince existing community resources to alter their services or work together to address an unmet need
    B. To gather and distribute information to consumers and agencies about unmet needs

C. To publicize existing community resources and make them more accessible
D. To bring an unmet community need to public attention in order to achieve acceptance of and support for fulfilling the need

17. Research in community outreach shows that women often build friendships through shared positive feelings, whereas men often build friendships through
    A. metacommunication
    B. catharsis
    C. impression management
    D. shared activities

18. Typically, the FIRST step in a community-needs assessment is to
    A. identify community's strengths
    B. explore the nature of the neighborhood
    C. get to know the area and its residents
    D. talk to people in the community

19. Most public relations experts agree that _____ exposure(s) to a message is the minimum just to get the message noticed. If the aim of a public outreach campaign is action or a change in behavior, the agency budget must plan for more exposures.
    A. one
    B. two
    C. three
    D. four

20. In the program development/community liaison model of community work and public outreach, the PRIMARY constituency is considered to be
    A. community representatives and the service agency board or administrators
    B. elected officials, social agencies, and interagency organizations
    C. marginalized or oppressed population groups in a city or region
    D. residents of a neighborhood, parish or rural county

21. Social or interpersonal problems in many African-American communities have their roots in
    A. personality deficits
    B. unresolved family conflicts
    C. poor communication
    D. external stressors

22. A public outreach campaign should
    I. focus on short-term, measurable goals, rather than ultimate outcomes
    II. try to alter entrenched attitudes within a short time, with powerfully worded messages
    III. proceed in steps or phases, each of which lays out a mechanism that leads to the desired effect
    IV. ignore causes that led to a problem, and instead focus on solutions

    The CORRECT answer is:
    A. I and II
    B. II and III
    C. III only
    D. I, II, III and IV

23. Research findings indicate that in listing preferences for helping professional attributes, individuals from culturally diverse groups are MOST likely to consider _____ as more important than _____.
    A. personality similarity; either race/ethnic similarity or attitude similarity
    B. therapist experience; any kind of similarity
    C. race/ethnic similarity; attitude similarity
    D. attitude similarity; race/ethnic similarity

24. Each of the following is considered to be an objective of community organization EXCEPT
    A. effecting changes in the distribution of decision-making power
    B. helping people develop and strengthen the traits of self-direction and cooperation
    C. effecting and maintaining the balance between needs and resources in a community
    D. helping people deal with their problems by developing alternative behaviors

25. A specialist is helping the adult protective services agency to design a public outreach campaign. The topic to be addressed is complex, public understanding is low, and most professionals at the agency feel that having more complete information might change the opinions of community members. Which method of pre-campaign research is probably MOST appropriate?
    A. Deliberative polling
    B. Attitude scales
    C. Surveys or questionnaires
    D. Focus groups

KEY (CORRECT ANSWERS)

1.	C	11.	C
2.	A	12.	A
3.	A	13.	B
4.	C	14.	B
5.	C	15.	C
6.	A	16.	B
7.	A	17.	D
8.	D	18.	B
9.	C	19.	C
10.	A	20.	A

21. D
22. C
23. D
24. D
25. A

TEST 2

DIRECTIONS: Each question or incomplete statement is followed by several suggested answers or completions. Select the one that BEST answers the question or completes the statement. *PRINT THE LETTER OF THE CORRECT ANSWER IN THE SPACE AT THE RIGHT.*

1. A specialist has been called in to resolve a dispute between two community leaders who have been arguing about the level of service needed within the community. The discussion has been going on for several hours when the specialist arrives, and both people seem to be upset.
After calming the two down and getting each of them to agree on a statement of the problem, the specialist should ask each person to
   A. summarize his or her argument in three main points
   B. explain why he or she became so upset
   C. clearly state, in objective terms, the position of the other in a form that meets with the other's approval
   D. identify the best alternative outcome, other than their presumed ideal

   1.____

2. In evaluating the impact of a public outreach campaign, the _____ model can be used early in the campaign to address first impressions.
   A. exposure or advertising
   B. expert interview
   C. impact monitoring or process
   D. experimental or quasi-experimental

   2.____

3. When trying to motivate an older population to take action on a community problem, it is helpful to remember that older people
   A. are more self-reliant in their decision-making than other members of the same family
   B. often need more time to decide than younger people
   C. are more likely than younger people to view community problems self-referentially
   D. tend to take a pragmatic, rather than philosophical, view of life

   3.____

4. The method of group or community decision-making that is normally MOST time-consuming is
   A. majority opinion   B. consensus
   C. expert opinion   D. authority rule

   4.____

5. A local adult protective services agency has identified one of the goals of its recent public outreach campaign to be the mobilization of activists.
The campaign should probably
   A. target neutral audiences
   B. home in on supporters
   C. stick to purely factual information
   D. try to persuade community fence-sitters

   5.____

6. Research of Native American youths' perceptions of family concerns for their well-being has generally found that these youths
   A. have a high degree of uncertainty about their families' feelings toward them
   B. believe their families don't care about them
   C. believe that their mothers care a great deal about them, but their fathers don't
   D. believe their families care a great deal about them

7. A domestic violence specialist is developing a new outreach program for the local community. The specialist has defined the target problem, set program goals, and planned the actions that will take place as a result of the program. Most likely, the next step will be to
   A. evaluate the resources available to achieve program goals
   B. define and sequence the steps that will be taken to achieve program goals
   C. determine how the program will be evaluated
   D. decide how the program will operate

8. Elder: *I'm so glad to have someone to talk to, someone who really understands my problem.*
   Specialist: *It is nice to be able to talk to someone who will listen.*
   Elder: *That's for sure.*
   In the above exchange, what listening skill is evident in the underlined statement?
   A. Verbatim response
   B. Paraphrasing
   C. Advising
   D. Evaluation

9. Which of the following activities is involved in the specialist's task of mobilizing?
   A. Meeting individuals in the community with problems and assisting them in finding help
   B. Identifying unmet community needs
   C. Speaking out against an unjust policy or procedure
   D. Developing new services or linking presently available services to meet community needs

10. The preliminary research associated with a public outreach campaign should FIRST be aimed at determining
    A. the budget
    B. the message's ultimate audience
    C. what media to use
    D. the short-term behavioral goals of the campaign

11. A specialist in a low-income community wants to plan programs that will deal with the influence of unemployment on domestic disturbances. The specialist needs to know not only how many unemployed people are in the community now, but also how many people will be unemployed at any particular tie in the future, and how those numbers will vary given certain conditions.

Probably the BEST way to trace employment rates over time and within differing conditions is through the use of
- A. the critical path
- B. linear programming
- C. difference equations
- D. the Markov model

12. Generally, public outreach programs—whatever their stated goal—should
    I. create a sense of urgency about a problem
    II. decline to identify opponents of the issue or idea
    III. propose concrete, easily understandable solutions
    IV. urge a specific action

    The CORRECT answer is:
    A. I only   B. I, III and IV   C. II and III   D. I, II, III and IV

13. Which of the following methods of community needs assessment relies to the GREATEST degree on existing public records?
    - A. Social indicators
    - B. Field study
    - C. Rates under treatment
    - D. Key informant

14. During an interview with a Native American client, a specialist is careful to maintain close and nearly constant eye contact.
    The client is MOST likely to interpret this as a(n)
    - A. show of high concern
    - B. sign of disrespect
    - C. uncomfortable assumption of intimacy
    - D. attempt to intimidate

15. The BEST strategy for addressing an audience that is known to be captive, or even hostile, is to
    - A. refer to experiences in common
    - B. flatter the audience
    - C. joke about things in or near the audience
    - D. plead for fairness

16. Integrative conflict resolution is characterized by
    - A. an overriding concern to maximize joint outcomes
    - B. one side's interests opposing the other's
    - C. a fixed and limited amount of resources to be divided, so that the more one group gets, the less another gets
    - D. manipulation and withholding information as negotiation strategies

17. A specialist wants to learn how to interact with the members of a largely Latino community in a more culturally sensitive way.
    Which of the following is NOT a guideline for interacting with members of a Latino community?
    - A. Efforts to foster independence and self-reliance may be interpreted by many Latinos as a lack of concern for others.
    - B. Efforts to deal one-on-one with an adolescent client may serve to alienate the parents, especially the mother.

C. A nonverbal gesture, such as lowering the eyes, is interpreted by many Latinos as a sign of respect and deference to authority.
D. In much of Latino culture, the focus of control for problems tends to be much more external than internal.

18. Each of the following is a supporting assumption of community organization, EXCEPT:
    A. Democracy requires cooperative participation.
    B. In order for communities to change, it is necessary for each individual in the community to be willing to change.
    C. Communities often need help with organization and planning.
    D. Holistic approaches work better than fragmented or ad-hoc programs.

18.____

19. Helping professionals often have difficulty to bring community resources together to fulfill unmet community needs.
    Which of the following is NOT usually a reason for this?
    A. Some community groups resist assistance when it is offered.
    B. Few community groups make their needs known.
    C. Community resources frequently change the type of services they offer.
    D. Often, community resources prefer to work alone.

19.____

20. When dealing with groups or populations of elderly clients, specialists should be mindful that about _____ of the nation's elderly suffer from mental health problems.
    A. a tenth   B. a quarter   C. a third   D. half

20.____

21. In an African-American community, a specialist from another culture should recognize that church participation, for most African-Americans, is viewed as a
    A. method for maintaining control and communicating competency
    B. way of depersonalizing problems or troubles
    C. way to divert attention away from problems
    D. means of cathartic emotional release

21.____

22. Adult protective service programs supported by state statutes protect elderly people from abuse and neglect under the doctrine of
    A. parens patriac   B. habeas corpus
    C. in loco parentis   D. volenti non fit injuria

22.____

23. In terms of public outreach, which of the following statements about an audience is NOT generally true?
    A. The more heterogeneous the audience, the more necessary it will be to use specific examples and appeals to certain types of people.
    B. The smaller the audience, the more likely that its members will share assumptions and values.
    C. When the speaker does not know the status of an audience, it is best to assume that they are captive rather than voluntary.
    D. The larger an audience, the more formal a presentation is likely to be.

23.____

24. A specialist often spends time in the places frequented by community residents. She listens carefully to what residents seem most concerned about, and engages many in conversations, asking them how they see the problems in the community. During these conversations, she makes mental notes about whether the statements of the problems are the same things that are mentioned in their conversations. From these conversations, the worker determines what she thinks the unmet needs of the community are.
    Which of the key issues in identifying unmet needs has the worker neglected to address?
    A. The different points of view regarding the issues, and whether there is any common ground
    B. Whether the stated problems and conversations with community residents reflect the same concerns
    C. How community residents define the issues
    D. What the residents talk about with one another in a community

25. Which of the following political styles should be used to promote an issue that could become controversial if it is perceived to involve major reforms?
    A. High-conflict, polarized
    B. High-conflict, consensual
    C. Moderate conflict, compromise-oriented
    D. Low-conflict, technical

KEY (CORRECT ANSWERS)

1. C
2. A
3. B
4. B
5. B

6. D
7. A
8. B
9. D
10. B

11. D
12. B
13. A
14. B
15. A

16. A
17. D
18. B
19. C
20. B

21. D
22. A
23. A
24. A
25. D

PREPARING WRITTEN MATERIAL

PARAGRAPH REARRANGEMENT
COMMENTARY

The sentences that follow are in scrambled order. You are to rearrange them in proper order and indicate the letter choice containing the correct answer at the space at the right.

Each group of sentences in this section is actually a paragraph presented in scrambled order. Each sentence in the group has a place in that paragraph; no sentence is to be left out. You are to read each group of sentences and decide upon the best order in which to put the sentences so as to form a well-organized paragraph.

The questions in this section measure the ability to solve a problem when all the facts relevant to its solution are not given.

More specifically, certain positions of responsibility and authority require the employee to discover connection between events sometimes, apparently, unrelated. In order to do this, the employee will find it necessary to correctly infer that unspecified events have probably occurred or are likely to occur. This ability becomes especially important when action must be taken on incomplete information.

Accordingly, these questions require competitors to choose among several suggested alternatives, each of which presents a different sequential arrangement of the events. Competitors must choose the MOST logical of the suggested sequences.

In order to do so, they may be required to draw on general knowledge to infer missing concepts or events that are essential to sequencing the given events. Competitors should be careful to infer only what is essential to the sequence. The plausibility of the wrong alternatives will always require the inclusion of unlikely events or of additional chains of events which are NOT essential to sequencing the given events.

It's very important to remember that you are looking for the best of the four possible choices, and that the best choice of all may not even be one of the answers you're given to choose from.

There is no one right way to solve these problems. Many people have found it helpful to first write out the order of the sentences, as they would have arranged them, on their scrap paper before looking at the possible answers. If their optimum answer is there, this can save them some time. If it isn't, this method can still give insight into solving the problem. Others find it most helpful to just go through each of the possible choices, contrasting each as they go along. You should use whatever method feels comfortable and works for you.

While most of these types of questions are not that difficult, we've added a higher percentage of the difficult type, just to give you more practice. Usually there are only one or two questions on this section that contain such subtle distinctions that you're unable to answer confidently. And you then may find yourself stuck deciding between two possible choices, neither of which you're sure about.

EXAMINATION SECTION

TEST 1

DIRECTIONS: The following groups of sentences need to be arranged in an order that makes sense. Select the letter preceding the sequence that represents the BEST sentence order. *PRINT THE LETTER OF THE CORRECT ANSWER IN THE SPACE AT THE RIGHT.*

1.
   I. The keyboard was purposely designed to be a little awkward to slow typists down.
   II. The arrangement of letters on the keyboard of a typewriter was not designed for the convenience of the typist.
   III. Fortunately, no one is suggesting that a new keyboard be designed right away.
   IV. If one were, we would have to learn to type all over again.
   V. The reason was that the early machines were slower than the typists and would jam easily.
   The CORRECT answer is:
   A. I, III, IV, II, V
   B. II, V, I, IV, III
   C. V, I, II, III, IV
   D. II, I, V, III, IV

   1.____

2.
   I. The majority of the new service jobs are part-time or low-paying.
   II. According to the U.S. Bureau of Labor Statistics, jobs in the service sector constitute 72% of all jobs in this country.
   III. If more and more workers receive less and less money, who will buy the goods and services needed to keep the economy going?
   IV. The service sector is by far the fastest growing part of the United States economy.
   V. Some economists look upon this trend with great concern.
   The CORRECT answer is:
   A. II, IV, I, V, III
   B. II, III, IV, I, V
   C. V, IV, II, III, I
   D. III, I, II, IV, V

   2.____

3.
   I They can also affect one's endurance.
   II. This can stabilize blood sugar levels, and ensure that the brain is receiving a steady, constant, supply of glucose, so that one is *hitting on all cylinders* while taking the test.
   III. By food, we mean real food, not junk food or unhealthy snacks.
   IV. For this reason, it is important not to skip a meal, and to bring food with you to the exam.
   V. One's blood sugar levels can affect how clearly one is able to think and concentrate during an exam.
   The CORRECT answer is:
   A. V, IV, II, III, I
   B. V, II, I, IV, III
   C. V, I, IV, III, II
   D. V, IV, I, III, II

   3.____

4. I. Those who are the embodiment of desire are absorbed in material quests, and those who are the embodiment of feeling are warriors who value power more than possession.
    II. These qualities are in everyone, but in different degrees.
    III. But those who value understanding yearn not for goods or victory, but for knowledge.
    IV. According to Plato, human behavior flows from three main sources: desire, emotion, and knowledge.
    V. In the perfect state, the industrial forces would produce but not rule, the military would protect but not rule, and the forces of knowledge, the philosopher kings, would reign.
    The CORRECT answer is:
    A. IV, V, I, II, III
    B. V, I, II, III, IV
    C. IV, III, II, I, V
    D. IV, II, I, III, V

5. I. Of the more than 26,000 tons of garbage produced daily in New York City, 12,000 tons arrive daily at Fresh Kills.
    II. In a month, enough garbage accumulates there to fill the Empire State Building.
    III. In 1937, the Supreme Court halted the practice of dumping the trash of New York City into the sea.
    IV. Although the garbage is compacted, in a few years the mounds of garbage at Fresh Kills will be the highest points south of Maine's Mount Desert Island on the Eastern Seaboard.
    V. Instead, tugboats now pull barges of much of the trash to Staten Island and the largest landfill in the world, Fresh Kills.
    The CORRECT answer is:
    A. III, V, IV, I, II
    B. III, V, II, IV, I
    C. III, V, I, II, IV
    D. III, II, V, IV, I

6. I. Communists rank equality very high, but freedom very low.
    II. Unlike communists, conservatives place a high value on freedom and a very low value on equality.
    III. A recent study demonstrated that one way to classify people's political beliefs is to look at the importance placed on two words: freedom and equality.
    IV. Thus, by demonstrating how members of these groups feel about the two words, the study has proved to be useful for political analysts in several European countries.
    V. According to the study, socialists and liberals rank both freedom and equality very high, while fascists rate both very low.
    The CORRECT answer is:
    A. III, V, I, II, IV
    B. V, IV, III, I, II
    C. III, V, IV, II, I
    D. III, I, II, IV, V

7.
I. "Can there be anything more amazing than this?"
II. If the riddle is successfully answered, his dead brothers will be brought back to life.
III. "Even though man sees those around him dying every day," says Dharmaraj, "he still believes and acts as if he were immortal."
IV. "What is the cause of ceaseless wonder?" asks the Lord of the Lake.
V. In the ancient epic, The Mahabharata, a riddle is asked of one of the Pandava brothers.
The CORRECT answer is:
A. V, II, I, IV, III
B. V, IV, III, I, II
C. V, II, IV, III, I
D. V, II, IV, I, III

8.
I. On the contrary, the two main theories—the cooperative (neoclassical) theory and the radical (labor theory)—clearly rest on very different assumptions, which have very different ethical overtones.
II. The distribution of income is the primary factor in determining the relative levels of material well-being that different groups or individuals attain.
III. Of all issues in economics, the distribution of income is one of the most controversial.
IV. The neoclassical theory tends to support the existing income distribution (or minor changes), while the labor theory ends to support substantial changes in the way income is distributed.
V. The intensity of the controversy reflects the fact that different economic theories are not purely neutral, *detached* theories with no ethical or moral implications.
The CORRECT answer is:
A. II, I, V, IV, III
B. III, II, V, I, IV
C. III, V, II, I, IV
D. III, V, IV, I, II

9.
I. The pool acts as a broker and ensures that the cheapest power gets used first.
II. Every six seconds, the pool's computer monitors all of the generating stations in the state and decides which to ask for more power and which to cut back.
III. The buying and selling of electrical power is handled by the New York Power Pool in Guilderland, New York.
IV. This is to the advantage of both the buying and selling utilities.
V. The pool began operation in 1970, and consists of the state's eight electric utilities.
The CORRECT answer is:
A. V, I, II, III, IV
B. IV, II, I, III, V
C. III, V, I, IV, II
D. V, III, IV, II, I

10. I. Modern English is much simpler grammatically than Old English.
    II. Finnish grammar is very complicated; there are some fifteen cases, for example.
    III. Chinese, a very old language, may seem to be the exception, but it is the great number of characters/words that must be mastered that makes it so difficult to learn, not its grammar.
    IV. The newest literary language—that is, written as well as spoken—is Finish, whose literary roots go back only to about the middle of the nineteenth century.
    V. Contrary to popular belief, the longer a language is been in use the simpler its grammar—not the reverse.
    The CORRECT answer is:
    A. IV, I, II, III, V
    B. V, I, IV, II, III
    C. I, II, IV, III, V
    D. IV, II, III, I, V

10.____

KEY (CORRECT ANSWERS)

1. D   6. A
2. A   7. C
3. C   8. B
4. D   9. C
5. C   10. B

TEST 2

DIRECTIONS: This type of question tests your ability to recognize accurate paraphrasing, well-constructed paragraphs, and appropriate style and tone. It is important that the answer you select contains only the facts or concepts given in the original sentences. It is also important that you be aware of incomplete sentences, inappropriate transitions, unsupported opinions, incorrect usage, and illogical sentence order. Paragraphs that do not include all the necessary facts and concepts, that distort them, or that add new ones are not considered correct.

The format for this section may vary. Sometimes, long paragraphs are given, and emphasis is placed on style and organization. Our first five questions are of this type. Other times, the paragraphs are shorter, and there is less emphasis on style and more emphasis on accurate representation of information. Our second group of five questions are of this nature.

For each of Questions 1 through 10, select the paragraph that BEST expresses the ideas contained in the sentences above it. *PRINT THE LETTER OF THE CORRECT ANSWER IN THE SPACE AT THE RIGHT.*

1.
   I. Listening skills are very important for managers.
   II. Listening skills are not usually emphasized.
   III. Whenever managers are depicted in books, manuals or the media, they are always talking, never listening.
   IV. We'd like you to read the enclosed handout on listening skills and to try to consciously apply them this week.
   V. We guarantee they will improve the quality of your interactions.

   1.____

   A. Unfortunately, listening skills are not usually emphasized for managers. Managers are always depicted as talking, never listening. We'd like you to read the enclosed handout on listening skills. Please try to apply these principles this week. If you do, we guarantee they will improve the quality of your interactions.
   B. The enclosed handout on listening skills will be important improving the quality of your interactions. We guarantee it. All you have to do is take sometime this week to read and to consciously try to apply the principles Listening skills are very important for manages, but they are not usually emphasized. Whenever managers are depicted in books, manuals or the media, they are always talking, never listening.
   C. Listening well is one of the most important skills a manager can have, yet it's not usually given much attention. Think about any representation of managers in books, manuals, or in the media that you may have seen. They're always talking, never listening. We'd like you to read the enclosed handout on listening skills and consciously try to apply them the rest of the week. We guarantee you will see a difference in the quality of your interactions.

101

D. Effective listening, one very important tool in the effective manager's arsenal, is usually not emphasized enough. The usual depiction of managers in books, manuals or the media is one in which they are always talking, never listening. We'd like you to read the enclosed handout and consciously try to apply the information contained therein throughout the rest of the week. We feel sure that you will see a marked difference in the quality of your interactions.

2. I. Chekhov wrote three dramatic masterpieces which share certain themes and formats: Uncle Vanya, The Cherry Orchard, and The Three Sisters.
   II. They are primarily concerned with the passage of time and how this erodes human aspirations.
   III. The plays are haunted by the ghosts of the wasted life.
   IV. The characters are concerned with life's lesser problems; however, such as the inability to make decisions, loyalty to the wrong cause, and the inability to be clear.
   V. This results in sweet, almost aching, type of a sadness referred to as Chekhovian.

2.____

   A. Chekhov wrote three dramatic masterpieces: Uncle Vanya, The Cherry Orchard, and The Three Sisters. These masterpieces share certain themes and formats: the passage of time, how time erodes human aspirations, and the ghosts of wasted life. Each masterpiece is characterized by a sweet, almost aching, type of sadness that has become known as Chekhovian. The sweetness of this sadness hinges on the fact that it is not the great tragedies of life which are destroying these characters, but their minor flaws: indecisiveness, misplaced loyalty, unclarity.
   B. The Cherry Orchard, Uncle Vanya, and The Three Sisters are three dramatic masterpieces written by Chekhov that use similar formats to explore a common theme. Each is primarily concerned with the way that passing time wears down human aspirations, and each is haunted by the ghosts of the wasted life. The characters are shown struggling futilely with the lesser problems of life: indecisiveness, loyalty to the wrong cause, and the inability to be clear. These struggles create a mood of sweet, almost aching, sadness that has become known as Chekhovian.
   C. Chekhov's dramatic masterpieces are, along with The Cherry Orchard, Uncle Vanya, and The Three Sisters. These plays share certain thematic and formal similarities. They are concerned most of all with the passage of time and the way in which time erodes human aspirations. Each play is haunted by the specter of the wasted life. Chekhov's characters are caught, however, by life's lesser snares: indecisiveness, loyalty to the wrong cause, and unclarity. The characteristic mood is a sweet, almost aching type of sadness that has come to be known as Chekhovian.
   D. A Chekhovian mood is characterized by sweet, almost aching, sadness. The term comes from three dramatic tragedies by Chekhov which revolve around the sadness of a wasted life. The three masterpieces (Uncle Vanya, The Three Sisters, and The Cherry Orchard) share the same

theme and format. The plays are concerned with how the passage of time erodes human aspirations. They are peopled with characters who are struggling with life's lesser problems. These are people who are indecisive, loyal to the wrong causes, or are unable to make themselves clear.

3. I. Movie previews have often helped producers decide which parts of movies they should take out or leave in.
    II. The first 1933 preview of King Kong was very helpful to the producers because many people ran screaming from the theater and would not return when four men first attacked by Kong were eaten by giant spiders.
    III. The 1950 premiere of Sunset Boulevard resulted in the filming of an entirely new beginning, and a delay of six months in the film's release.
    IV. In the original opening scene, William Holden was in a morgue talking with thirty-six other "corpses" about the ways some of them had died.
    V. When he began to tell them of his life with Gloria Swanson, the audience found this hilarious, instead of taking the scene seriously.

    3.____

    A. Movie previews have often helped producers decide what parts of movies they should leave in or take out. For example, the first preview of King Kong in 1933 was very helpful. In one scene, four men were first attacked by Kong and then eaten by giant spiders. Many members of the audience ran screaming from the theater and would not return. The premiere of the 1950 film Sunset Boulevard was also very helpful. In the original opening scene, William Holden was in a morgue with thirty-six other "corpses," discussing the ways some of them had died. When he began to tell them of his life with Gloria Swanson, the audience found this hilarious. They were supposed to take the scene seriously. The result was a delay of six months in the release of the film while a new beginning was added.
    B. Movie previews have often helped producers decide whether they should change various parts of a movie. After the 1933 preview of King Kong, a scene in which four men who had been attacked by Kong were eaten by giant spiders was taken out as many people ran screaming from the theater and would not return. The 1950 premiere of Sunset Boulevard also led to some changes. In the original opening scene, William Holden was in a morgue talking with thirty-six other "corpses" about the ways some of them had died. When he began to tell them of his life with Gloria Swanson, the audience found this hilarious, instead of taking the scene seriously.
    C. What do Sunset Boulevard and King Kong have in common? Both show the value of using movie previews to test audience reaction. The first 1933 preview of King Kong showed that a scene showing four men being eaten by giant spiders after having been attacked by Kong was too frightening for many people. They ran screaming from the theater and couldn't be coaxed back. The 1950 premiere of Sunset Boulevard was also a scream, but not the kind the producers intended. The movie opens

with William Holden lying in a morgue discussing the ways they had died with thirty-six other "corpses." When he began to tell them of his life with Gloria Swanson, the audience couldn't take him seriously. Their laughter caused a six-month delay while the beginning was rewritten.

D. Producers very often use movie previews to decide if changes are needed. The premiere of <u>Sunset Boulevard</u> in 1950 led to a new beginning and a six-month delay in film release. At the beginning, William Holden and thirty-six other "corpses" discuss the ways some of them died. Rather than taking this seriously, the audience thought it was hilarious when he began to tell them of his life with Gloria Swanson. The first 1933 preview of <u>King Kong</u> was very helpful for its producers because one scene so terrified the audience that many of them ran screaming from the theater and would not return. In this particular scene, four men who had first been attacked by Kong were eaten by giant spiders.

4. I. It is common for supervisors to view employees as "things" to be manipulated. 4.____
    II. This approach does not motivate employees, nor does the carrot-and-stick approach because employees often recognize these behaviors and resent them.
    III. Supervisors can change these behaviors by using self-inquiry and persistence.
    IV. The best managers genuinely respect those they work with, are supportive and helpful, and are interested in working as a team with those they supervise.
    V. They disagree with the Golden Rule that says "he or she who has the gold makes the rules."

    A. Some managers act as if they think the Golden Rule means "he or she who has the gold makes the rules." They show disrespect to employees by seeing them as "things" to be manipulated. Obviously, this approach does not motivate employees any more than the carrot-and-stick approach motivates them. The employees are smart enough to spot these behaviors and resent them. On the other hand, the managers genuinely respect those they work with, are supportive and helpful, and are interested in working as a team. Self-inquiry and persistence can change even the former type of supervisor into the latter.
    B. Many supervisors all into the trap of viewing employees as "things" to be manipulated, or try to motivate them by using a carrot-and-stick approach. These methods do not motivate employees, who often recognize the behaviors and resent them. Supervisors can change these behaviors, however, by using self-inquiry and persistence. The best managers are supportive and helpful, and have genuine respect for those with whom they work. They are interested in working as a team with those they supervise. To them, the Golden Rule is not "he or she who has the gold makes the rules."
    C. Some supervisors see employees as "things" to be used or manipulated using a carrot-and-stick technique. These methods don't work. Employees often see through them and resent them. A supervisor who

wants to change may do so. The techniques of self-inquiry and persistence can be used to turn him or her into the type of supervisor who doesn't think the Golden Rule is "he or she who has the gold makes the rules." They may become like the best managers who treat those with whom they work with respect and give them help and support. These are the manager who know how to build a team.

D. Unfortunately, many supervisors act as if their employees are objects whose movements they can position at will. This mistaken belief has the same result as another popular motivational technique—the carrot-and-stick approach. Both attitudes can lead to the same result—resentment from those employees who recognize the behaviors for what they are. Supervisors who recognize these behaviors can change through the use of persistence and the use of self-inquiry. It's important to remember that the best managers respect their employees. They readily give necessary help and support and are interested in working as a team with those they supervise. To these managers, the Golden Rule is not "he or she who has the gold makes the rules."

5. I. The first half of the nineteenth century produced a group of pessimistic poets—Byron, De Musset, Heine, Pushkin, and Leopardi.
II. It also produced a group of pessimistic composers—Schubert, Chopin, Schumann, and even the later Beethoven.
III. Above all, in philosophy, there was the profoundly pessimistic philosopher, Schopenhauer.
IV. The Revolution was dead, the Bourbons were restored, the feudal barons were reclaiming their land, and progress everywhere was being suppressed, as the great age was over.
V. "I thank God," said Goethe, "that I am not young in so thoroughly finished a world."

5.____

A. "I thank God," said Goethe, "that I am not young in so thoroughly finished a world." The Revolution was dead, the Bourbons were restored, the feudal barons were reclaiming their land, and progress everywhere was being suppressed. The first half of the nineteenth century produced a group of pessimistic poets: Byron, De Musset, Heine, Pushkin, and Leopardi. It also produced pessimistic composers: Schubert, Chopin, Schumann. Although Beethoven came later, he fits into this group, too. Finally and above all, it also produced a profoundly pessimistic philosopher, Schopenhauer. The great age was over.

B. The first half of the nineteenth century produced a group of pessimistic poets: Byron, De Musset, Heine, Pushkin, and Leopardi. It produced a group of pessimistic composers: Schubert, Chopin, Schumann, and even the later Beethoven. Above all, it produced a profoundly pessimistic philosopher, Schopenhauer. For each of these men, the great age was over. The Revolution was dead, and the Bourbons were restored. The feudal barons were reclaiming their land, and progress everywhere was being suppressed.

C. The great age was over. The Revolution was dead—the Bourbons were restored, and the feudal barons were reclaiming their land. Progress everywhere was being suppressed. Out of this climate came a profound pessimism. Poets, like Byron, De Musset, Heine, Pushkin, and Leopardi; composers, like Schubert, Chopin, Schumann, and even the later Beethoven; and above all, a profoundly pessimistic philosopher, Schopenauer. This pessimism which arose in the first half of the nineteenth century is illustrated by these words of Goethe, "I thank God that I am not young in so thoroughly finished a world."

D. The first half of the nineteenth century produced a group of pessimistic poets, Byron, De Musset, Heine, Pushkin, and Leopardi—and a group of pessimistic composers, Schubert, Chopin, Schumann, and the later Beethoven. Above it all, it produced a profoundly pessimistic philosopher, Schopenhauer. The great age was over. The Revolution was dead, the Bourbons were restored, the feudal barons were reclaiming their land, and progress everywhere was being suppressed. "I thank God," said Goethe, "that I am not young in so thoroughly finished a world."

6. I. A new manager sometimes may feel insecure about his or her competence in the new position.
   II. The new manager may then exhibit defensive or arrogant behavior towards those one supervises, or the new manager may direct overly flattering behavior toward one's new supervisor.

   A. Sometimes, a new manager may feel insecure about his or her ability to perform well in this new position. The insecurity may lead him or her to treat others differently. He or she may display arrogant or defensive behavior towards those he or she supervises, or be overly flattering to his or her new supervisor.
   B. A new manager may sometimes feel insecure about his or her ability to perform well in the new position. He or she may then become arrogant, defensive, or overly flattering towards those he or she works with.
   C. There are times when a new manager may be insecure about how well he or she can perform in the new job. The new manager may also behave defensive or act in an arrogant way towards those he or she supervises, or overly flatter his or her boss.
   D. Sometimes a new manager may feel insecure about his or her ability to perform well in the new position. He or she may then display arrogant or defensive behavior towards those they supervise, or become overly flattering towards their supervisors.

7. I. It is possible to eliminate unwanted behavior by bringing it under stimulus control—tying the behavior to a cue, and then never, or rarely, giving the cue.
   II. One trainer successfully used this method to keep an energetic young porpoise from coming out of her tank whenever she felt like it, which was potentially dangerous.
   III. Her trainer taught her to do it for a reward, in response to a hand signal, and then rarely gave the signal.

6.____

7.____

A. Unwanted behavior can be eliminated by tying the behavior to a cue, and then never, or rarely, giving the cue. This is called stimulus control. One trainer was able to use this method to keep an energetic young porpoise from coming out of her tank by teaching her to come out for a reward in response to a hand signal, and then rarely giving the signal.
B. Stimulus control can be used to eliminate unwanted behavior. In this method, behavior is tied to a cue, and then the cue is rarely, if ever, given. One trainer was able to successfully use stimulus control to keep an energetic young porpoise from coming out of her tank whenever she felt like it—a potentially dangerous practice. She taught the porpoise to come out for a reward when she gave a hand signal, and then rarely gave the signal.
C. It is possible to eliminate behavior that is undesirable by bringing it under stimulus control by tying behavior to a signal, and then rarely giving the signal. One trainer successfully used this method to keep an energetic porpoise from coming out of her tank, a potentially dangerous situation. Her trainer taught the porpoise to do it for a reward, in response to a hand signal, and then would rarely give the signal.
D. By using stimulus control, it is possible to eliminate unwanted behavior by tying the behavior to a cue, and then rarely or never give the cue. One trainer was able to use this method to successfully stop a young porpoise from coming out of her tank whenever she felt like it. To curb this potentially dangerous practice, the porpoise was taught by the trainer to come out of the tank for a reward, in response to a hand signal, and then rarely given the signal.

8. I. There is a great deal of concern over the safety of commercial trucks, caused by their greatly increased role in serious accidents since federal deregulation in 1981.
   II. Recently, 60 percent of trucks in New York and Connecticut and 70 percent of trucks in Maryland randomly stopped by state troopers failed safety inspections.
   III. Sixteen states in the United States require no training at all for truck drivers.

   8.____

   A. Since federal deregulation in 1981, there has been a great deal of concern over the safety of commercial trucks, and their greatly increased role in serious accidents. Recently, 60 percent of trucks in New York and Connecticut, and 70 percent of trucks in Maryland failed safety inspections. Sixteen states in the United States require no training at all for truck drivers.
   B. There is a great deal of concern over the safety of commercial trucks since federal deregulation in 1981. Their role in serious accidents has greatly increased. Recently, 60 percent of trucks randomly stopped in Connecticut and New York and 70 percent in Maryland failed safety inspections conducted by state troopers. Sixteen states in the United States provide no training at all for truck drivers.
   C. Commercial trucks have a greatly increased role in serious accidents since federal deregulation in 1981. This has led to a great deal of concern.

Recently, 70 percent of trucks in Maryland and 60 percent of trucks in New York and Connecticut failed inspection of those that were randomly stopped by state troopers. Sixteen states in the United States require no training for all truck drivers.

D. Since federal deregulation in 1981, the role that commercial trucks have played in serious accidents has greatly increased, and this has led to a great deal of concern. Recently, 60 percent of trucks in New York and Connecticut, and 70 percent of trucks in Maryland randomly stopped by state troopers failed safety inspections. Sixteen states in the U.S. don't require any training for truck drivers.

9.
I. No matter how much some people have, they still feel unsatisfied and want more, or want to keep what they have forever.
II. One recent television documentary showed several people flying from New York to Paris for a one-day shopping spree to buy platinum earrings, because they were bored.
III. In Brazil, some people were ordering coffins that cost a minimum of $45,000 and are equipping them with deluxe stereos, televisions, and other graveyard necessities.

9.____

A. Some people, despite having a great deal, still feel unsatisfied and want more, or think they can keep what they have forever. One recent documentary on television showed several people enroute from Paris to New York for a one day shopping spree to buy platinum earrings, because they were bored. Some people in Brazil are even ordering coffins equipped with such graveyard necessities as deluxe stereos and televisions. The price of the coffins start at $45,000.
B. No matter how much some people have, they may feel unsatisfied. This leads them to want more, or to want to keep what they have forever. Recently, a television documentary depicting several people flying from New York to Paris for a one day shopping spree to buy platinum earrings. They were bored. Some people in Brazil are ordering coffins that cost at least $45,000 and come equipped with deluxe televisions, stereos and other necessary graveyard items.
C. Some people will be dissatisfied no matter how much they have. They may want more, or they may want to keep what they have forever. One recent television documentary showed several people, motivated by boredom, jetting from New York to Paris for a one-day shopping spree to buy platinum earrings. In Brazil, some people are ordering coffins equipped with deluxe stereos, televisions and other graveyard necessities. The minimum price for these coffins—$45,000.
D. Some people are never satisfied. No matter how much they have they still want more, or think they can keep what they have forever. One television documentary recently showed several people flying from New York to Paris for the day to buy platinum earrings because they were bored. In Brazil, some people are ordering coffins that cost $45,000 and are equipped with deluxe stereos, televisions and other graveyard necessities.

9 (#2)

10.
- I. A television signal or video signal has three parts.
- II. Its parts are the black-and-white portion, the color portion, and the synchronizing (sync) pulses, which keep the picture stable.
- III. Each video source, whether it's a camera or a video-cassette recorder contains its own generator of these synchronizing pulses to accompany the picture that it's sending in order to keep it steady and straight.
- IV. In order to produce a clean recording, a video-cassette recorder must "lock-up" to the sync pulses that are part of the video it is trying to record, and this effort may be very noticeable if the device does not have gunlock.

10.____

A. There are three parts to a television or video signal: the black-and-white part, the color part, and the synchronizing (sync) pulses, which keep the picture stable. Whether it's a video-cassette recorder or a camera, each video source contains its own pulse that synchronizes and generates the picture it's sending in order to keep it straight and steady. A video-cassette recorder must "lock up" to the sync pulses that are part of the video it's trying to record. If the device doesn't have gunlock, this effort must be very noticeable.

B. A video signal or television is comprised of three parts: the black-and-white portion, the color portion, and the sync (synchronizing) pulses, which keep the picture stable. Whether it's a camera or a video-cassette recorder, each video source contains its own generator of these synchronizing pulses. These accompany the picture that it's sending in order to keep it straight and steady. A video-cassette recorder must "lock up" to the sync pulses that are part of the video it is trying to record in order to produce a clean recording. This effort may be very noticeable if the device does not have gunlock.

C. There are three parts to a television or video signal: the color portion, the black-and-white portion, and the sync (synchronizing pulses). These keep the picture stable. Each video source, whether it's a video-cassette recorder or a camera, generates these synchronizing pulses accompanying the picture it's sending in order to keep it straight and steady. If a clean recording is to be produced, a video-cassette recorder must store the sync pulses that are part of the video it is trying to record. This effort may not be noticeable if the device does not have gunlock.

D. A television signal or video signal has three parts: the black-and-white portion, the color portion, and the synchronizing (sync) pulses. It's the sync pulses which keep the picture stable, which accompany it and keep it steady and straight. Whether it's a camera or a video-cassette recorder, each video source contains its own generator of these synchronizing pulses. To produce a clean recording, a video-cassette recorder must "lock up" to the sync pulses that are part of the video it is trying to record. If the device does not have gunlock, this effort may be very noticeable.

KEY (CORRECT ANSWERS)

1. C
2. B
3. A
4. B
5. D
6. A
7. B
8. D
9. C
10. D

PREPARING WRITTEN MATERIAL
EXAMINATION SECTION
TEST 1

DIRECTIONS: Each of the sentences in this test may be classified under one of the following four categories:
- A. Faulty because of incorrect grammar or word usage
- B. Faulty because of incorrect punctuation
- C. Faulty because of incorrect capitalization or incorrect spelling
- D. Correct

Examine each sentence carefully to determine under which of the above four options it is best classified. Then, in the space to the right, print the capital letter preceding the option which is the BEST of the four suggested above. (Note that each faulty sentence contains but one type of error. Consider a sentence to be correct if it contains none of the types of errors mentioned, even though there may be other correct ways of expressing the same thought.)

1. He sent the notice to the clerk who you hired yesterday. 1.____
2. It must be admitted, however that you were not informed of this change. 2.____
3. Only the employee who have served in this grade for at least two years are eligible for promotion. 3.____
4. The work was divided equally between she and Mary. 4.____
5. He thought that you were not available at that time. 5.____
6. When the messenger returns; please give him this package. 6.____
7. The new secretary prepared, typed, addressed, and delivered, the notices. 7.____
8. Walking into the room, his desk can be seen at the rear. 8.____
9. Although John has worked here longer than She, he produces a smaller amount of work. 9.____
10. She said she could of typed this report yesterday. 10.____
11. Neither one of these procedures are adequate for the efficient performance of this task. 11.____
12. The typewriter is the tool of the typist; the cash register, the tool of the cashier. 12.____

13. "The assignment must be completed as soon as possible" said the supervisor. 13._____

14. As you know, office handbooks are issued to all new Employees. 14._____

15. Writing a speech is sometimes easier than to deliver it before an audience. 15._____

16. Mr. Brown our accountant, will audit the accounts next week. 16._____

17. Give the assignment to whomever is able to do it most efficiently. 17._____

18. The supervisor expected either your or I to file these reports. 18._____

KEY (CORRECT ANSWERS)

1.	A	11.	A
2.	B	12.	C
3.	D	13.	B
4.	A	14.	C
5.	D	15.	A
6.	B	16.	B
7.	B	17.	A
8.	A	18.	A
9.	C		
10.	A		

TEST 2

DIRECTIONS: Each of the sentences in this test may be classified under one of the following four categories:
- A. Faulty because of incorrect grammar or word usage
- B. Faulty because of incorrect punctuation
- C. Faulty because of incorrect capitalization or incorrect spelling
- D. Correct

Examine each sentence carefully to determine under which of the above four options it is best classified. Then, in the space to the right, print the capital letter preceding the option which is the BEST of the four suggested above. (Note that each faulty sentence contains but one type of error. Consider a sentence to be correct if it contains none of the types of errors mentioned, even though there may be other correct ways of expressing the same thought.)

1. The fire apparently started in the storeroom, which is usually locked.   1.____
2. On approaching the victim, two bruises were noticed by this officer.   2.____
3. The officer, who was there examined the report with great care.   3.____
4. Each employee in the office had a seperate desk.   4.____
5. All employees including members of the clerical staff, were invited to the lecture.   5.____
6. The suggested Procedure is similar to the one now in use.   6.____
7. No one was more pleased with the new procedure than the chauffeur.   7.____
8. He tried to persaude her to change the procedure.   8.____
9. The total of the expenses charged to petty cash were high.   9.____
10. An understanding between him and I was finally reached.   10.____

KEY (CORRECT ANSWERS)

1.	D	6.	C
2.	A	7.	D
3.	B	8.	C
4.	C	9.	A
5.	B	10.	A

TEST 3

DIRECTIONS: Each of the sentences in this test may be classified under one of the following four categories:
- A. Faulty because of incorrect grammar or word usage
- B. Faulty because of incorrect punctuation
- C. Faulty because of incorrect capitalization or incorrect spelling
- D. Correct

Examine each sentence carefully to determine under which of the above four options it is best classified. Then, in the space to the right, print the capital letter preceding the option which is the BEST of the four suggested above. (Note that each faulty sentence contains but one type of error. Consider a sentence to be correct if it contains none of the types of errors mentioned, even though there may be other correct ways of expressing the same thought.)

1. They told both he and I that the prisoner had escaped.   1.____

2. Any superior officer, who, disregards the just complaint of his subordinates, is remiss in the performance of his duty.   2.____

3. Only those members of the national organization who resided in the Middle West attended the conference in Chicago.   3.____

4. We told him to give the national organization assignment to whoever was available.   4.____

5. Please do not disappoint and embarass us by not appearing in court.   5.____

6. Although the office's speech proved to be entertaining, the topic was not relevent to the main theme of the conference.   6.____

7. In February all new officers attended a training course in which they were learned in their principal duties and the fundamental operating procedure of the department.   7.____

8. I personally seen inmate Jones threaten inmates Smith and Green with bodily harm if they refused to participate in the plot.   8.____

9. To the layman, who on a chance visit to the prison observes everything functioning smoothly, the maintenance of prison discipline may seem to be a relatively easily realizable objective.   9.____

10. The prisoners in cell block fourty were forbidden to sit on the cell cots during the recreation hour.   10.____

KEY (CORRECT ANSWERS)

1. A 6. C
2. B 7. A
3. C 8. A
4. D 9. D
5. C 10. C

TEST 4

DIRECTIONS: Each of the sentences in this test may be classified under one of the following four categories:
- A. Faulty because of incorrect grammar or word usage
- B. Faulty because of incorrect punctuation
- C. Faulty because of incorrect capitalization or incorrect spelling
- D. Correct

Examine each sentence carefully to determine under which of the above four options it is best classified. Then, in the space to the right, print the capital letter preceding the option which is the BEST of the four suggested above. (Note that each faulty sentence contains but one type of error. Consider a sentence to be correct if it contains none of the types of errors mentioned, even though there may be other correct ways of expressing the same thought.)

1. I cannot encourage you any.   1._____
2. You always look well in those sort of clothes.   2._____
3. Shall we go to the park?   3._____
4. The man whome he introduced was Mr. Carey.   4._____
5. She saw the letter laying here this morning.   5._____
6. It should rain before the Afternoon is over.   6._____
7. They have already went home.   7._____
8. That Jackson will be elected is evident.   8._____
9. He does not hardly approve of us.   9._____
10. It was he, who won the prize.   10._____

KEY (CORRECT ANSWERS)

1.	A	6.	C
2.	A	7.	A
3.	D	8.	D
4.	C	9.	A
5.	A	10.	B

TEST 5

DIRECTIONS: Each of the sentences in this test may be classified under one of the following four categories:
- A. Faulty because of incorrect grammar or word usage
- B. Faulty because of incorrect punctuation
- C. Faulty because of incorrect capitalization or incorrect spelling
- D. Correct

Examine each sentence carefully to determine under which of the above four options it is best classified. Then, in the space to the right, print the capital letter preceding the option which is the BEST of the four suggested above. (Note that each faulty sentence contains but one type of error. Consider a sentence to be correct if it contains none of the types of errors mentioned, even though there may be other correct ways of expressing the same thought.)

1. Shall we go to the park.   1.____
2. They are, alike, in this particular way.   2.____
3. They gave the poor man sume food when he knocked on the door.   3.____
4. I regret the loss caused by the error.   4.____
5. The students' will have a new teacher.   5.____
6. They sweared to bring out all the facts.   6.____
7. He decided to open a branch store on 33rd street.   7.____
8. His speed is equal and more than that of a racehorse.   8.____
9. He felt very warm on that Summer day.   9.____
10. He was assisted by his friend, who lives in the next house.   10.____

KEY (CORRECT ANSWERS)

1.	B	6.	A
2.	B	7.	C
3.	C	8.	A
4.	D	9.	C
5.	B	10.	D

TEST 6

DIRECTIONS: Each of the sentences in this test may be classified under one of the following four categories:
- A. Faulty because of incorrect grammar or word usage
- B. Faulty because of incorrect punctuation
- C. Faulty because of incorrect capitalization or incorrect spelling
- D. Correct

Examine each sentence carefully to determine under which of the above four options it is best classified. Then, in the space to the right, print the capital letter preceding the option which is the BEST of the four suggested above. (Note that each faulty sentence contains but one type of error. Consider a sentence to be correct if it contains none of the types of errors mentioned, even though there may be other correct ways of expressing the same thought.)

1. The climate of New York is colder than California. 1.____
2. I shall wait for you on the corner. 2.____
3. Did we see the boy who, we think, is the leader. 3.____
4. Being a modest person, John seldom talks about his invention. 4.____
5. The gang is called the smith street bos. 5.____
6. He seen the man break into the store. 6.____
7. We expected to lay still there for quite a while. 7.____
8. He is considered to be the Leader of his organization. 8.____
9. Although I recieved an invitation, I won't go. 9.____
10. The letter must be here some place. 10.____

KEY (CORRECT ANSWERS)

1.	A	6.	A
2.	D	7.	A
3.	B	8.	C
4.	D	9.	C
5.	C	10.	A

TEST 7

DIRECTIONS: Each of the sentences in this test may be classified under one of the following four categories:
- A. Faulty because of incorrect grammar or word usage
- B. Faulty because of incorrect punctuation
- C. Faulty because of incorrect capitalization or incorrect spelling
- D. Correct

Examine each sentence carefully to determine under which of the above four options it is best classified. Then, in the space to the right, print the capital letter preceding the option which is the BEST of the four suggested above. (Note that each faulty sentence contains but one type of error. Consider a sentence to be correct if it contains none of the types of errors mentioned, even though there may be other correct ways of expressing the same thought.)

1. I though it to be he. 1.____
2. We expect to remain here for a long time. 2.____
3. The committee was agreed. 3.____
4. Two-thirds of the building are finished. 4.____
5. The water was froze. 5.____
6. Everyone of the salesmen must supply their own car. 6.____
7. Who is the author of Gone With the Wind? 7.____
8. He marched on and declaring that he would never surrender. 8.____
9. Who shall I say called? 9.____
10. Everyone has left but they. 10.____

KEY (CORRECT ANSWERS)

1. A   6. A
2. D   7. B
3. D   8. A
4. A   9. D
5. A   10. D

TEST 8

DIRECTIONS: Each of the sentences in this test may be classified under one of the following four categories:
- A. Faulty because of incorrect grammar or word usage
- B. Faulty because of incorrect punctuation
- C. Faulty because of incorrect capitalization or incorrect spelling
- D. Correct

Examine each sentence carefully to determine under which of the above four options it is best classified. Then, in the space to the right, print the capital letter preceding the option which is the BEST of the four suggested above. (Note that each faulty sentence contains but one type of error. Consider a sentence to be correct if it contains none of the types of errors mentioned, even though there may be other correct ways of expressing the same thought.)

1. Who did we give the order to?   1.____
2. Send your order in immediately.   2.____
3. I believe I paid the Bill.   3.____
4. I have not met but one person.   4.____
5. Why aren't Tom, and Fred, going to the dance?   5.____
6. What reason is there for him not going?   6.____
7. The seige of Malta was a tremendous event.   7.____
8. I was there yesterday I assure you   8.____
9. Your ukulele is better than mine.   9.____
10. No one was there only Mary.   10.____

KEY (CORRECT ANSWERS)

1. A   6. A
2. D   7. C
3. C   8. B
4. A   9. C
5. B   10. A

TEST 9

DIRECTIONS: In each of the following groups of sentences, one of the four sentences is faulty in grammar, punctuation, or capitalization. Select the INCORRECT sentence in each case.

1. A. If you had stood at home and done your homework, you would not have failed in arithmetic.
   B. Her affected manner annoyed every member of the audience.
   C. How will the new law affect our income taxes?
   D. The plants were not affected by the long, cold winter, but they succumbed to the drought of summer.

2. A. He is one of the most able men who have been in the Senate.
   B. It is he who is to blame for the lamentable mistake.
   C. Haven't you a helpful suggestion to make at this time?
   D. The money was robbed from the blind man's cup.

3. A. The amount of children in this school is steadily increasing.
   B. After taking an apple from the table, she went out to play.
   C. He borrowed a dollar from me.
   D. I had hoped my brother would arrive before me.

4. A. Whom do you think I hear from every week?
   B. Who do you think is the right man for the job?
   C. Who do you think I found in the room?
   D. He is the man whom we considered a good candidate for the presidency.

5. A. Quietly the puppy laid down before the fireplace.
   B. You have made your bed; now lie in it.
   C. I was badly sunburned because I had lain too long in the sun.
   D. I laid the doll on the bed and left the room.

KEY (CORRECT ANSWERS)

1. A
2. D
3. A
4. C
5. A

HOUSING AND COMMUNITY DEVELOPMENT GLOSSARY

ACRONYMS AND ABBREVIATED REFERENCES

ACC	Annual contributions contract.
AHOP	Areawide housing opportunity plan.
AHS	Annual housing survey.
AML	Adjustable mortgage loan.
APA	Administrative Procedure Act (5 U.S.C. 551 et seq.)
ARM	Adjustable rate mortgage.
BMIR	Below-market interest rate.
Budget Act	Congressional Budget and Impoundment Control Act of 1974.
Budget Res.	Concurrent resolution on the budget.
CBO	Congressional Budget Office.
CD	Community development.
CDBG	Community development block grant.
CFR	Code of Federal Regulations.
CIAP	Comprehensive improvement assistance program.
Continuing Res.	Joint resolution continuing appropriations for the next fiscal year.
CPI	Consumer Price Index.
DOE	Department of Energy.
EDA	Economic Development Administration.
EIS	Environmental impact statement.
ERTA	Economic Recovery Tax Act of 1981.
Fannie Mae	Federal National Mortgage Association.
FDIC	Federal Deposit Insurance Corporation.
FEMA	Federal Emergency Management Agency.
FFB	Federal Financing Bank.
FHA	Federal Housing Administration.
FHLBB	Federal Home Loan Bank Board.
FHLMC	Federal Home Loan Mortgage Corporation (Freddie Mac).
FmHA	Farmers Home Administration.
FMR	Fair market rent.
FNMA	Federal National Mortgage Association (Fannie Mae).
FR	Federal Register.
Freddie Mac	Federal Home Loan Mortgage Corporation.
FSLIC	Federal Savings and Loan Insurance Corporation.
GAO	Government Accounting Office.
Garn-St Germain	Garn-St Germain Depository Institutions Act of 1982.
GEM	Growing equity mortgage.
Ginnie Mae	Government National Mortgage Association.
GNMA	Government National Mortgage Association (Ginnie Mae).

GLOSSARY

GPM	Graduated payment mortgage.
Gramm-Latta	Omnibus Budget Reconciliation Act of 1981.
HAP	Housing assistance plan.
HFA	Housing finance agency.
HHS	Department of Health and Human Services.
HoDAG	Housing development grant.
HUD	Department of Housing and Urban Development.
HURRA	Housing and Urban-Rural Recovery Act of 1983.
IG	Inspector General.
IRS	Internal Revenue Service.
MBS	Mortgage-backed securities.
Mod Rehab	Moderate rehabilitation.
MPS	Minimum property standards.
MSA	Metropolitan statistical area.
NHP	National Housing Partnership.
NIBS	National Institute of Building Sciences.
NOFA	Notice of funding availability.
NSA	Neighborhood strategy area.
OBRA	Omnibus Budget Reconciliation Act of 1981.
OMB	Office of Management and Budget.
PAM	Pledged account mortgage.
PC	Participation certificate.
PFS	Performance funding system.
PHA	Public housing agency.
PLAM	Price-level adjusted mortgage.
PMI	Private mortgage insurance.
PUD	Planned unit development.
RAM	Reverse annuity mortgage.
RAP	Rental assistance payments.
REIT	Real estate investment trust.
RESPA	Real Estate Settlement Procedures Act of 1974.
SAM	Shared appreciation mortgage.
Solar Bank	Solar Energy and Energy Conservation Bank.
SRO	Single room occupancy housing.
Sub Rehab	Substantial rehabilitation.
TEFRA	Tax Equity and Fiscal Responsibility Act of 1982.
TMAP	Temporary mortgage assistance payments.
UDAG	Urban development action grant.
U.S.C	United States Code.
VA	Veterans' Administration.

ABBREVIATED STATUTORY CITATIONS

Sec. 5	United States Housing Act of 1937 (funding for public housing and section 8 housing).
Sec. 7(o)	Department of Housing and Urban Development Act (legislative review of HUD rules and regulations).

GLOSSARY

Sec. 8	United States Housing Act of 1937 (low-income rental housing assistance).
Sec. 9	United States Housing Act of 1937 (operating subsidies).
Sec. 14	United States Housing Act of 1937 (CLAP).
Sec. 17	United States Housing Act of 1937 (rental rehabilitation and development).
Sec. 101	Housing and Urban Development Act of 1965 (rent supplement).
Sec. 104	Housing and Community Development Act of 1974 (CDBG applications and review).
Sec. 105	Housing and Community Development Act of 1974 (CDBG eligible activities).
Sec. 106	Housing and Community Development Act of 1974 (CDBG allocation and distribution of funds).
Sec. 107	Housing and Community Development Act of 1974 (CD discretionary fund).
Sec. 108	Housing and Community Development Act of 1974 (CD loan guarantees).
Sec. 119	Housing and Community Development Act of 1974 (UDAG).
Sec. 201	Housing and Community Development Amendments of 1978 (troubled projects).
Sec. 202	Housing Act of 1959 (elderly and handicapped housing).
Sec. 203	Housing and Community Development Amendments of 1978 (management and preservation of HUD-owned projects). National Housing Act (single-family mortgage insurance).
Sec. 207	National Housing Act (multifamily mortgage insurance).
Sec. 213	Housing and Community Development Act of 1974 (allocation of funds for assisted housing). National Housing Act (cooperative housing mortgage insurance).
Sec. 221	National Housing Act (multifamily mortgage insurance).
Sec. 221(d)(3)	National Housing Act (BMIR rental housing mortgage insurance).
Sec. 231	National Housing Act (mortgage insurance for elderly and handicapped rental housing).
Sec. 235	National Housing Act (home mortgage interest reduction payments).
Sec. 236	National Housing Act (rental and cooperative housing interest reduction payments).
Sec. 302(b)(2)	Federal National Mortgage Association Charter Act (FNMA authority to deal in conventional mortgages).

GLOSSARY

Sec. 305(a)(2)	Federal Home Loan Mortgage Corporation Act (FHLMC authority to deal in conventional mortgages).
Sec. 312	Housing Act of 1964 (rehabilitation loans).
Sec. 502	Housing Act of 1949 (rural housing loans and loan guarantees).
Sec. 513	Housing Act of 1949 (rural housing authorization amounts).
Sec. 515	Housing Act of 1949 (elderly and handicapped rural housing).
Sec. 521	Housing Act of 1949 (rural housing loan interest credits and RAP).
Sec. 533	Housing Act of 1949 (housing preservation grants).
Title I	Housing and Community Development Act of 1974 (CDBG and UDAG). Housing Act of 1949 (urban renewal). National Housing Act (FHA property improvement loan insurance).
Title II	National Housing Act (FHA mortgage insurance).
Title V	Housing Act of 1949 (rural housing).

TERMS

Adjustable mortgage loan—See "adjustable rate mortgage".

Adjustable rate mortgage—A mortgage covering a loan the interest rate of which may vary periodically over the term of the loan, generally according to an established index. Also referred to as an adjustable mortgage loan.

Amortization—Gradual reduction of the principal of a loan, together with the payment of interest, according to a schedule of periodic payments so that the principal is fully paid by the end of the term of the loan.

Annual contributions contract—A contract under which HUD makes payments to a public housing agency equal to the amount of principal and interest owed by the PHA under obligations issued by it for the development, operation, or modernization of a public housing project.

Annual housing survey—An annual study by HUD and the Bureau of the Census regarding housing units, homeowners, and renters.

Appropriation—Constitutionally required legislation that grants Federal agencies the authority to make payments out of the Treasury for general or particular purposes. There are three general categories of appropriations legislation: general, supplemental, and continuing.

Areawide housing opportunity plan—A program to reduce the geographical concentration of lower income families by expanding housing opportunities throughout a wide area.

Assistance payments—Federal payments, made directly or through public housing agencies, to owners or prospective owners of rental housing to pay part of the rent of lower income tenants. See "interest-reduction payments".

Assumable mortgage—Mortgage in which the existing debt may be taken over by a third party without approval of the lender.

GLOSSARY

Authorization—Legislation granting authority for the congressional consideration of appropriations for general or particular purposes. Although unauthorized appropriations may be subject to points of order, they are legally valid if enacted.

Balloon mortgage—Mortgage under which the loan matures before the principal is fully repaid.

Below-market interest rate—HUD-insured mortgages financing homes for lower income families and displaced families bearing interest rates lower than the market rate, with the Federal Government bearing the cost of the difference in rates by purchase of the mortgages. See section 221(d)(3) of the National Housing Act.

Block grants—Grants by HUD on a noncategorical formula basis to assist community development and rehabilitation, including slum and blight elimination, conservation of housing, increased public services, improved use of land, and preservation of property. See title I of the Housing and Community Development Act of 1974.

Borrowing authority—Authority to incur indebtedness for which the Federal Government is liable, which authority is granted in advance of the provision of appropriations to repay such debts. Borrowing authority may take the form of authority to borrow from the Treasury or authority to borrow from the public by means of the sale of Federal agency obligations. Borrowing authority is not an appropriation since it provides a Federal agency only with the authority to incur a debt, and not the authority to make payments from the Treasury under the debt. Subsequent appropriations are required to liquidate the borrowing authority.

Budget authority—Legal authority to enter into obligations that will result in immediate or future outlays of Federal funds. Appropriations (unless liquidating borrowing authority or contract authority), contract authority, and borrowing authority are the three primary types of budget authority.

Coinsurance—HUD insurance of a mortgage, advance, or loan with the lender assuming a percentage of the loss on the insured obligation. See section 244 of the National Housing Act.

Commitment—An agreement to make or purchase a mortgage loan at a future date, or an agreement to insure a mortgage at a future date, if prescribed conditions are met by the mortgagee. Under HUD mortgage insurance, a traditional administration distinction exists between a special type of commitment known as a "conditional commitment" and other commitments known as "firm commitments". Under the former, a commitment is made to insure a mortgage (on a specific property for a definite loan amount) to be given by a future purchaser of the property involved if such a purchaser meets certain eligibility requirements. The term "standby commitment" is commonly used in the secondary market for residential mortgages to describe a commitment to purchase a mortgage loan or loans with specific terms, both parties understanding that the purchase is not likely to be completed unless particular circumstances make that advantageous to the seller of the mortgage. These commitments are typically used to enable the borrower to obtain construction financing at a lower cost on the assumption that permanent financing of the project will be available on more favorable terms than under the commitment when the project is completed and generating income.

Community development block grants—Block grants for community development made to States, urban counties, and metropolitan cities under section 106 of the Housing and Community Development Act of 1974.

GLOSSARY

Comprehensive improvement assistance—Assistance provided for the modernization of public housing projects under section 14 of the United States Housing Act of 1937.

Concurrent resolution on the budget—Concurrent resolution of the Congress establishing minimum revenues and maximum outlays for the congressional budget for the Federal Government.

Conditional commitment—See "commitment".

Condominiums—Multifamily housing projects with individual units owned by occupants, who also own an undivided interest in the common areas and facilities of the project.

Contract authority—Authority to enter into contracts obligating the Federal Government to make payments in the future, which authority is granted in advance of the provision of appropriations to make such payments. Contract authority is not an appropriation since it provides a Federal agency only with the authority to incur an obligation, and not the authority to make payments from the Treasury under the obligation. Subsequent appropriations are required to liquidate the contract authority.

Conventional mortgage—A mortgage covering a loan that is not insured by the HUD or guaranteed by the FmHA or VA.

Cooperatives—Multifamily housing projects owned by cooperative corporations with the stockholders of the corporations having the right to occupancy of the units.

Cost certification—A limitation, under HUD mortgage insurance for multifamily housing, on the amount of a mortgage eligible for insurance, which limitation is determined after completion of the project on the basis of the builder's certification as to the actual dollar amount of his costs for specific items of construction and prescribed related expenditures. Under this requirement, the insured mortgage is limited to a fixed percentage of that certified amount.

Deep subsidy program—Program of rental assistance payments under section 236(f)(2) of the National Housing Act.

Default—Failure to meet the terms of a mortgage or other loan agreement. Generally, a delinquency of more than 30 days under a mortgage is considered a default.

Delinquency—Failure to make any timely payment due under a mortgage or other loan agreement.

Direct endorsement—HUD program of delegated private mortgage processing of FHA loan applications under the single family mortgage insurance programs.

Discount point—An amount that may be payable to a lender by a borrower or seller in addition to principal and interest, equal to 1 percent of the principal amount of the loan.

Discretionary fund—Funds set aside for discretionary grants by HUD under section 107 of the Housing and Community Development Act of 1974.

Due-on-sale clause—A clause that may be included in a mortgage to authorize the mortgagee to require full repayment of the loan upon any transfer of the property.

Economic mix—Occupancy of rental housing by families of varying economic levels, including very low-income families, which is to be promoted by housing assistance payments. See section 8 of the United States Housing Act of 1937.

Elderly and handicapped housing—Generally refers to housing for elderly and handicapped persons developed by nonprofit sponsors with assistance provided by HUD under section 202 of the Housing Act of 1959.

GLOSSARY

Entitlement community—An urban county or metropolitan city eligible to receive a community development block grant directly from HUD.

Environmental impact statements—Statements required to be made under section 102(2)(C) of the National Environmental Policy Act of 1969 by Federal agencies in their recommendations or reports on proposals for legislation and other major Federal actions significantly affecting the quality of the human environment, as to the environmental impact of the proposed action; any adverse environmental effects that cannot be avoided should the proposal be implemented; relationship between local short-term use of man's environment and the maintenance and enhancement of long-term productivity; and any irreversible or irretrievable commitments of resources that would be involved in the proposed action should it be implemented. Applicants for block grants can assume responsibility for this statement under the community development program. See section 104(f) of the Housing and Community Development Act of 1974.

Estimated value—The basis of one of the limits on the amount of a mortgage that can be insured by HUD. For example, under certain programs the mortgage may not exceed 90 percent of the estimated value of the property when completed.

Fair market rent—An amount determined by HUD to be the cost of modest rental units in a particular market area.

Federal Home Loan Mortgage Corporation—A federally established and sponsored corporation, under the supervision of the Federal Home Loan Bank Board, that provides a secondary market primarily for conventional mortgages.

Federal Housing Administration—Part of HUD that has responsibility for carrying out the mortgage insurance programs of the National Housing Act.

Federal National Mortgage Association—A federally established and sponsored private corporation, under the general supervision of HUD, that provides a secondary market for mortgages.

Firm commitment—See "commitment".

Fiscal year—Annual accounting period of the Federal Government, beginning October 1 and ending September 30 of the subsequent calendar year. The fiscal year is designated by the calendar year in which it ends, so that fiscal year 2005 refers to the fiscal year beginning October 1, 2004 and ending September 30, 2005.

Flood insurance program—Program under which FEMA makes flood insurance available to participating communities under the National Flood Insurance Act of 1968.

Forebearance—The act of postponing or refraining from taking legal action against a mortgagor even though mortgage payments are in arrears.

Foreclosure—Legal procedure under which the property securing a loan is sold to pay the debt owed by a borrower who has defaulted.

Government National Mortgage Association—Federal corporation, and part of HUD, that provides a secondary market for federally guaranteed mortgages.

Graduated payment mortgage—A mortgage under which payments are comparatively low initially and then increase over a specified period before reaching a constant level.

Ground lease—Lease of land without improvements.

Growing equity mortgage—Mortgage under which payments increase over a specified period in order to accelerate the repayment of principal and thereby shorten the term of the loan.

Guaranteed loan—Loan in which a private lender is assured repayment by the Federal Government of part or all of the principal or interest, or both, in the event of a

GLOSSARY

default by the borrower. Unlike an insured loan, no insurance fund exists and no insurance premiums are paid.

Hold-harmless provision—Statutory provision ensuring the continued eligibility of a specified class for certain assistance for a limited period of time. The most commonly cited examples are contained in paragraphs (4) and (6) of section 102(a) of the Housing and Community Development Act of 1974.

Home equity conversion mortgage—A form of mortgage in which the lender makes periodic payments to the borrower using the borrower's equity in the home as security.

Housing allowance payments—Payments made by HUD under section 504 of the Housing Act of 1970 to assist families in meeting rental or homeownership expenses.

Housing assistance plan—A part of the CDBG application describing local housing conditions and sets quantitative goals for providing housing to low- and moderate-income residents.

Housing development grant—Grant made by HUD under section 17(d) of the United States Housing Act of 1937 for the new construction or substantial rehabilitation of rental housing.

Housing finance agency—State agency responsible for financing housing and administering assisted housing programs.

Housing preservation grant—Grant made by FmHA under section 533 of the Housing Act of 1949 for the rehabilitation of single-family housing, rental housing, or cooperatives for low- and very low-income families and persons.

Industrial revenue bond—A debt instrument issued by a municipality or development corporation to finance the development of revenue-producing projects. Project revenues are then used to pay the debt service on the bonds. Section 103(b) of the Internal Revenue Code of 1954 establishes certain limitations.

Installment land contract—See "land contract".

Insured loan—Loan in which a private lender is assured repayment by the Federal Government of part or all of the principal or interest, or both, and for which the borrower pays insurance premiums.

Interest rate credits—Generally refers to the FmHA program of subsidized interest rate loans for single-family and multifamily housing for low or moderate income families under section 521(a)(1)(B) of the Housing Act of 1949. The subsidy may reduce the interest rate to as low as 1 percent.

Interest reduction payments—Periodic assistance payments by HUD to mortgagees to permit lower interest rate payments by lower income families (varying with fluctuations in incomes) on HUD insured mortgages financing homes, rental housing, or cooperative housing. See sections 235 and 236 of the National Housing Act.

Land contract—An agreement to transfer title to a property upon fulfillment of the contract conditions. Under an "installment land contract", the purchaser assumes possession immediately and makes periodic payments to the vendor (the owner of the property); title is transferred only when all payments have been made.

Leased housing—Low-rent housing provided by public housing agencies in housing leased from private owners.

Leveraging—The maximization of the effect of Federal assistance for a project by obtaining additional project funding from non-Federal sources. See section 119 of the Housing and Community Development Act of 1974.

Lien—Any legal claim on a property for payment of a debt. A mortgage is one example.

GLOSSARY

Loan-to-value ratio—The relationship between the amount of the mortgage loan and the appraised value of the property involved, expressed as a percentage of the appraised value. It is one of the traditional limitations on a mortgage eligible for mortgage insurance.

Lower income family—Generally, a family whose income does not exceed 80 percent of the median family income of the area involved.

Manufactured home—Housing, including a mobile home, that is factory-built or prefabricated.

Market rent—Rental that would be charged by the owner of a HUD-insured multifamily dwelling unit if the owner were paying interest on the loan at the HUD-approved market interest rate.

Metropolitan city—For purposes of the CDBG program, a city that is the central city of a metropolitan area or that has a population of not less than 50,000.

Metropolitan statistical area—Metropolitan area defined by the Office of Management and Budget. Previously referred to as standard metropolitan statistical area.

Minimum property standards—HUD regulations establishing minimum acceptable standards for properties to be purchased with HUD-insured mortgage loans.

Moderate income family—For purposes of the CDBG program, a family whose income exceeds 50 percent of the median family income of the area involved, but does not exceed 80 percent of the median family income of the area.

Moderate rehabilitation—Rehabilitation that is less comprehensive than substantial rehabilitation, such as repair or replacement of the heating or electrical system of a project.

Modernization—See "comprehensive improvement assistance".

Mortgage—Conveyance of an interest in real property as security for repayment of a loan, including a loan made for the purchase or improvement of the real property.

Mortgage-backed securities—Obligations issued by an organization that has held and set aside mortgages as security for payment of the obligations. FNMA, GNMA, and FHLMC, as well as private organizations, issue such obligations.

Mortgage insurance programs—Generally refers to the insured loan programs carried out by HUD, through the FHA, under the National Housing Act.

Mortgage revenue bonds—Tax-exempt bonds issued by State and local governments and agencies to finance the sale or repair of single-family housing. The bonds are payable from revenues derived from repayments of interest on the mortgage loans financed from the proceeds of the bonds. Section 103A of the Internal Revenue Code of 1954 establishes certain limitations. Referred to as mortgage subsidy bonds in the Internal Revenue Code of 1954.

Mortgagee—A lender who is conveyed an interest in real property under a mortgage.

Mortgagor—A borrower who conveys an interest in real property under a mortgage.

Multifamily housing—Generally a project containing dwelling units for more than 4 families.

National Housing Partnership—A private limited partnership established under title IX of the Housing and Urban Development Act of 1969 for the purpose of carrying out the building, maintenance, or rehabilitation of housing and related facilities for lower or moderate income families. It can enter into partnerships or joint ventures, conduct research, provide technical assistance, and make loans or grants to accomplish its purpose.

10

GLOSSARY

National Institute of Building Sciences—A nonprofit nongovernmental organization established under section 809 of the Housing and Community Development Act of 1974 to make findings and to advise public and private sectors of the economy with respect to the use of building science and technology in achieving nationally acceptable standards for use in housing and building regulations.

Negative amortization—A loan prepayment schedule under which payments do not cover the full amount of interest due. The unpaid interest is added to the principal and, as a result, the outstanding principal balance increases rather than decreases.

Neighborhood development grant—A grant made by HUD to an eligible neighborhood nonprofit organization under section 123 of the Housing and Urban-Rural Recovery Act of 1983 to assist the organization in carrying out certain neighborhood development activities.

Neighborhood strategy area—Area in which concentrated housing rehabilitation and community development block grant activities are being undertaken.

Nonentitlement area—For purposes of the CDBG program, an area that is neither a metropolitan city nor urban county, and is therefore generally ineligible for direct grants from HUD.

Nonprofit sponsor—A group organized to undertake a housing project for reasons other than making a profit.

Notice of funding availability—A notice by HUD to inform potential project sponsors that contract authority is available.

Off-budget program—Federal program the transactions of which are not included in the Budget of the United States Government as a result of statutory requirement.

Operating subsidies—HUD payments to public housing agencies to assist the payment of operating expenses of public housing, or to the owners of certain multifamily projects for low income families. See section 9 of the United States Housing Act of 1937.

Participation loan—Loans made by the FmHA or others when another lender makes part of the loan.

Pass through—Principal and interest receipts on housing mortgages are "passed through" by GNMA, FNMA, FHLMC, or other organizations to the purchasers of their securities or obligations that have been sold and secured by the mortgages set aside as security for the obligations.

Planned unit development—Development and construction of a residential community as a unit in accordance with a plan for the entire development.

Pledged account mortgage—A graduated payment mortgage in which part of the buyer's down payment is deposited in a savings account. Funds are drawn from the account to supplement the buyer's monthly payments during the early years of the loan.

Pocket of poverty—For purposes of the UDAG program, a contiguous area of particularly severe poverty in a city or urban county. A city or urban county that fails to meet the general eligibility standards for UDAG assistance may be eligible if it contains such an area.

Prepayment penalty—A penalty that may be levied for repayment of a loan before it falls due.

Price-level adjusted mortgage—Mortgage under which the outstanding balance is adjusted according to an established price index, while the interest rate remains fixed.

Principal—The amount of debt, exclusive of accrued interest, remaining on a loan. Before any principal has been repaid, the total loaned amount is the principal.

GLOSSARY

Private mortgage insurance—Insurance by private companies of lenders against losses on mortgage loans.

Program reservation—HUD action reserving funds for a specific approved public housing project. This reservation is subject to PHA fulfillment of all HUD requirements.

Public housing—Lower income housing owned and operated by a public housing agency and assisted under the United States Housing Act of 1937 (other than under section 8 or 17).

Public housing agency—Public agency established by a State or local government to finance or operate low-income housing assisted under the United States Housing Act of 1937.

Real estate investment trust—A trust established by real estate investors primarily for the management and control of investments in mortgages and to sell obligations secured by mortgages and property held by the trust.

Recapture—Requiring repayment of assistance provided, either because the assistance has not been used within a certain period of time or a specified event (such as the sale of assisted property) occurs that permits repayment of all or a part of the assistance. See section 235(c)(2) of the National Housing Act.

Refinancing—Payment of a loan with amounts borrowed under a new loan.

Rehabilitation—The improvement or repair of property. Such term includes substantial and moderate rehabilitation, but excludes new construction.

Rehabilitation loans—Loans made by HUD under section 312 of the Housing Act of 1964 for the rehabilitation of property.

Reinsurance—Program under section 249 of the National Housing Act to demonstrate possible advantages of having private mortgage insurance companies enter into reinsurance contracts with HUD, under which such private insurers would assume a percentage of the risk on certain single-family mortgages insured by HUD.

Rent control—Limitation of annual rent increases by municipal ordinance, State, or Federal law.

Rent supplements—Annual Federal payments to owners of housing built with certain HUD mortgage insurance on behalf of prescribed types of lower income families.

Rental assistance payments—Generally refers to the FmHA program of rental assistance for low income families in rural areas under section 521(a)(2)(A) of the Housing Act of 1949.

Replacement cost—The basis of one of the limits placed on the amount of a mortgage that can be insured by HUD under certain programs, such as the mortgage may not exceed 90 percent of replacement cost of the housing when completed.

Reverse annuity mortgage—See "home equity conversion mortgage".

Rural area—A non-urban area meeting the requirements of section 520 of the Housing Act of 1949 and eligible assistance under the FmHA housing programs.

Second mortgage—A mortgage that grants rights subordinate to the rights granted by the initial mortgage. A second mortgage generally bears a higher rate of interest than the initial mortgage to reflect the greater risk of the lender.

Secondary mortgage market—Nationwide market for the purchase and sale of mortgages. FHLMC, FNMA, and GNMA are the 3 federally established entities that purchase mortgages in the secondary mortgage market, thereby increasing the availabilty of funds to financial institutions for additional residential loans.

Seed money—Advances, loans, or grants to cover preliminary expenses of constructing housing projects, such as the cost of planning and obtaining financing.

GLOSSARY

Shared appreciation mortgage—Mortgage under which the borrower receives financial assistance in purchasing a property and agrees in return to give the lender a portion of the future increase in the value of the property.

Shared housing—Generally refers to arrangements under which elderly and handicapped persons share the facilities of a dwelling with others in order to meet their housing needs and reduce the costs of housing. See section 8(p) of the United States Housing Act of 1937.

Single-family housing—Generally a structure containing dwelling units for 1 to 4 families.

Single room occupancy housing—Residential properties in which some or all dwelling units do not contain bathroom or kitchen facilities. See section 8(n) of the United States Housing Act of 1937.

Small city—A city that does not qualify as a metropolitan city for purposes of receiving a community development block grant under section 106 of the Housing and Community Development Act of 1974.

Standby commitment—See "commitment".

Substantial rehabilitationImprovements of a property from substandard to safe and sanitary conditions. It can vary from gutting and reconstruction to accumulated deferred maintenance. It may also involve conversion of nonresidential property to residential use.

Supplemental loans—HUD-insured loans under section 241 of the National Housing Act for improvements or additions to multifam-ily housing, nursing homes, group practice facilities, or hospitals.

Tandem plan purchases—The purchase by GNMA of certain housing mortgages at higher prices than would be paid by FNMA, FHLMC or other mortgage purchasers, with subsequent resale by GNMA at the best price obtainable, or as back-up of GNMA's mortgage-backed securities. The term derives from the original practice of FNMA purchasing from GNMA "in tandem" with the GNMA purchase.

Temporary mortgage assistance payments—Mortgage assistance payments authorized to be made under section 230(a) of the National Housing Act to a mortgagor of a single-family residence who defaults on the mortgage due to circumstances beyond the mortgagor's control. Constitutes an alternative to acquisition of the mortgage by HUD under section 230(b) of the National Housing Act.

Tenant contribution—The monthly amount of rent required to be paid by a tenant receiving rental assistance under a Federal housing program. Currently is 30 percent of monthly adjusted family income. See section 3(a) of the United States Housing Act of 1937.

Total development costs—The sum of all HUD-approved costs for planning, administration, site acquisition, relocation, demolition, construction and equipment, interest and carrying charges, on-site streets and utilities, nondwelling facilities, a contingency allowance, insurance premiums, off-site facilities, any initial operating deficit, and all other costs necessary to develop the project.

Troubled housing—Rental or cooperative housing project receiving assistance from HUD under section 201 of the Housing and Community Development Amendments of 1978 to restore financial soundness, improve management, and maintain the low and moderate income character of the project.

GLOSSARY

Turnkey housing—Housing initially financed and built by private sponsors and purchased upon completion by public housing agencies for use by lower income families under the public housing program.

Unit of general local government—A general purpose political subdivision of a State, such as a county, city, township, town, or village.

Urban county—For purposes of the CDBG and UDAG programs, generally refers to a county in a metropolitan area that has a combined population of not less than 200,000.

Urban development action grant—A grant made to an urban county, city, or unincorporated portion of an urban county under section 119 of the Housing and Community Development Act of 1974.

Urban homesteading—Program of HUD transfers of unoccupied residences under section 810 of the Housing and Community Development Act of 1974 to individuals or families without any substantial consideration where the individuals or families agree to occupy the residences not less than 5 years and to make repairs and improvements required to meet health and safety standards within certain time limits. Under a demonstration multifamily homestead-ing program, HUD transfers properties to local governments for conversion or rehabilitation to use primarily as housing for lower income families.

Urban renewal—Elimination and prevention of the development or spread of slums and blight, including slum clearance and redevelopment, or rehabilitation and conservation, assisted by HUD advances, loans, and grants under title I of the Housing Act of 1949. Program is being terminated under the provisions of title I of the Housing and Community Development Act of 1974.

Usury laws—Laws limiting the maximum rate of interest that may be charged on a loan.

Vacancy rate—In reference to dwelling units, the percentage of the total dwelling units in an area that are vacant and available for residence.

Variable interest rate—A means by which a lender is permitted to adjust the interest rate on a loan to reflect changes in the prime rateusually within a prescribed range and with advanced notice.

Very low-income family—Generally, a family whose income does not exceed 50 percent of the median family income of the area involved.

Voucher demonstration—Demonstration program of rental assistance under section 8(o) of the United States Housing Act of 1937. Assistance payments are provided for an eligible family based on the difference between the payment standard established by the Secretary for the area involved and 30 percent of the family's monthly adjusted income. The tenant contribution is the difference between the rent negotiated by the family and the amount of the monthly assistance payment.

www.ingramcontent.com/pod-product-compliance
Lightning Source LLC
Chambersburg PA
CBHW082207300426
44117CB00016B/2701